SCANDINAVIA

I NORWAY, ÅLESUND

SCANDINAVIA

EDITED BY
MARTIN HÜRLIMANN

TEXT BY
COUNT OXENSTIERNA

225 PHOTOGRAVURE PLATES
8 PLATES IN COLOR

A STUDIO BOOK
THE VIKING PRESS · NEW YORK

LIBRARY OF CONGRESS CATALOG CARD NUMBER : 63–12710
TEXT PRINTED IN GREAT BRITAIN BY JARROLD AND SONS LTD. NORWICH
GRAVURE PLATES PRINTED BY ETS BRAUN ET CIE. MULHOUSE, FRANCE
COLOR PLATES PRINTED BY IMAGO, ZURICH, SWITZERLAND

THE Scandinavian peoples are regarded by the rest of the world with great sympathy and respect. Their culture is ancient, their economy modern; they have three admirable Kings and a bevy of young Princesses; they also have two Presidents and a democratic tradition to which they are staunchly faithful. The Scandinavians are peace-lovers, though war has sometimes been thrust upon them. They have a background of scholarship and many of them have won international fame. To meet them is always a stimulating and delightful experience.

But mingling with all these tributes to the Scandinavian peoples one can often sense a faint irritation, if not a definitely critical attitude. One hears it asserted that, when all is said and done, they have not taken the trouble to build themselves into a great political and cultural union. They have preferred to continue as petty States; they are out of the European swim. Now that the European Community is being created they are making too many claims for special consideration, which are difficult to meet, and in any case they seem to have little inclination for spiritual or social integration. Judgments of this kind are so often encountered, in conversation or in print, that it seems high time to lay down a firm practical foundation for future discussions.

The Scandinavian family of nations might, indeed, serve as a model for a closer union among the European nations, for it offers the picture of a genuine community of peoples which, far from being on the decline, has now reached maturity and full individual development. At least three times in the course of history it has given a display of united strength. On the other hand it has had to endure endless struggles for power within its own borders. From all this its members have learnt independence yet association, self-denial and tolerance. Their co-operation is accepted without question, for it comes quite naturally to them. Their various national peculiarities and customs form no obstacle; on the contrary these are regarded as a source of enrichment; they help to foster and consolidate the subtle feeling of underlying unity. Scandinavia has thus achieved the maturity that the rest of Europe is still painfully struggling to attain. How this has come about, and what message Scandinavia has to convey, will be explained in the following pages and shown in the illustrations to this book.

Everybody feels at ease among the kindly Danes! They invariably greet the stranger with a friendly smile, even in the smallest of the farms that lie scattered over their gently rolling, fertile countryside. Here everything is spick and span, rambler roses climb up the walls of many of the houses and people are never too busy to sit down on the bench that stands beside nearly every door and enjoy a pleasant chat. Subjects for conversation are always at hand—the rippling cornfields, the cattle and pigs, the weather and the news in the papers. The Danes appear to live in perfect harmony with the friendly, fruitful land that their hands have partly shaped. But appearances are deceptive, as we shall soon discover.

A traveller arriving in Sweden from Denmark perceives no great change in scenery until he enters the extensive pine-forests through which the train carries him for hours. Here and there patches have been cleared and brought under the plough and the gleam of a hidden lake is seen at frequent intervals. But in most places the barren rubble left behind by the ice masses provides a foothold only for conifers; no other trees would produce sturdy timber on a diet of air, water and sunshine. And as the mountains gradually come into view, raising their peaks of primeval rock, granite or gneiss, the scene takes on an aspect that bears little or no resemblance to anything in central or southern Europe.

The German often takes a romantic view of his native land, reclaimed from the virgin forest by his ancestors, gentle yet positive. There, man and nature exercise a reciprocal influence on one another. Man lives amid nature, and only on rare occasions do the stern forces of storm, river and mountain assert their power. The Italian has a different attitude towards his land-scape, with its harmonious lines. Never would it occur to him to penetrate into the thick forests that clothe its steep mountains. They provide the backcloth before which his colourful life is acted.

This also explains the astonishment with which the Swedish painter Richard Bergh looked upon his native land when he returned there in 1890 after several years' study in southern Europe. 'The raggedness of Nature, the untidiness of it!' he exclaimed. 'Where is that architectural, picturesque unity that renders Nature in the South so enchanting to the artist, with its clear, well-ordered lines? Not here. Here your thirst for colour must be content with colourless black and white, your sense of form with a shapeless jumble. The whole scene is a chaotic confusion of tremendous, ponderous, oppressive monotony.'

Such were the harsh words of an artist arriving from the south. But he very soon succeeded in creating impressionistic pictures of this northern scenery. He and his contemporaries captured the magic light of the north, the bright aura of the northern sunrise, skies reflected in the lake waters and the solemnity of the dark forests. The Swedes and Finns began, on foot, to explore their natural surroundings, using skis and snowshoes. They put up their tents long before camping sites were heard of, they swam, they sunbathed, they built summer cottages by the sea or in the woods. And they discovered the majesty of nature in the northern part of their countries, where wooded heights and sparkling lakes stretch far and wide, where the soft dawn strengthens to the glow of the midnight sun, and where man must comply unquestioningly with the solemn dictates of winter.

As for the Norwegians, they had to settle on the narrow green ledges between mountain and fjord, building themselves log-houses in the midst of their pastures and ploughland. This was human territory, whereas in those early centuries the mountains belonged to Jotunheim, the home of the giants. Snorri tells us that a giantess lived there. Her name was Night; she had a daughter called Earth and a son called Day who was radiant and comely like his father, one of the gods. But there was another giantess, Angrbodr, and she bore three children—the wolf Fenrir, the world serpent (Midgardsormr), and Hel, goddess of the underworld. All the evil giants dwelt in Jotunheim, and were a sore trouble to the gods. The Vikings had much to tell of them, and so had the pious folk in medieval times.

Then there was Thjazi, who abducted the goddess of youth, so that the other gods of Asgardr began to grow old—a dreadful misfortune—before they at last managed to defeat him. His daughter came forward to avenge him and demanded compensation; this she received by marriage with one of the gods. Their union was by no means a happy one, for the god in question insisted on living by the sea, while the giantess would not leave the mountains where she spent her time ski-ing and hunting wild beasts. Her name was Skadi, and she bestowed it upon Skadin-auia, or Scandinavia—Skadi's meadow or island, which floats on the ocean just as *Orbis Terrarum*, the globe of the world, was believed by the ancients to float in the cosmic waters.

And everyone has heard of Dovrefjell, the home of the trolls visited by Peer Gynt. In a great hall in the mountain, the Old Man of Dovre dances with his subjects, 'who are sufficient unto themselves'. Thus it is that many people are believed to be changelings, troll-children, endowed with terrible powers of divination and with the dangerous urge to be '*seg self nok*'. The Norwegian imagination found a powerful stimulus in this contrast between the cramped reality of life on the fjords and the terrifying remoteness of the mountain peaks. For thousands of years they have related their sagas round the fire in the winter evenings. Not until the beginning of the nineteenth century did they begin to discover the beauties of their barren, tameless, perilous landscape. Then they were intoxicated by the magnificent play of line and colour. But only after their dormant sense of nationality was aroused did the Norwegians develop a direct and entirely personal relationship to their own country. Then only did its primitive natural forces begin to exert a real influence as one pole of a spiritual field of tension in everyday life. Then only was Norway ready for its great dramatists.

Railways extended into the mountains. People began to be less awed by the forces of nature. The majestic Jotunheim became comfortably accessible, and Scandinavia's highest mountain, Galdhøpiggen (8,097 feet), could be contemplated and climbed by whoever cared to do so. Sport became the universal, daily outlet for the Norwegians' national conscious-ness and enthusiasm for nature. Even the people of the capital flock out to enjoy their native surroundings on Sundays and on the dark winter evenings. Life there is fresher and closer to reality than in Sweden or Finland.

Last comes Iceland, the island within the Arctic circle, first discovered about the year 865. Here the early settlers found a fertile soil, geysers, hot springs, waterfalls, and mighty precipices under whose protecting shadow their *Althing* held its yearly meetings. These mighty phenomena have inspired their epic literature and quickened their imagination for the last thousand years. The Scandinavian feeling for nature takes a variety of forms, yet they all have a common foundation, quite distinct from that of the European lands further south.

7

The languages and dialects of Scandinavia are equally diverse, yet they are all parts of a general pattern. In the days of the Vikings the men who gathered aboard the dragon ships from all parts of the territory had no difficulty in understanding one another. This is clear from the two thousand runic stones which have come down to us. But even by the eleventh century the language was dividing into an eastern and a western branch. The geographical isolation that set in with the Middle Ages led by about 1300 to the formation of five separate dialects—Swedish, Danish, Norwegian, Faeroese and Icelandic. The linguistic unity of Scandinavia had been destroyed.

At the present time, we Scandinavians can understand one another across our national frontiers; we never have to learn one another's languages. But now and then we need to make an effort; some of the Norwegian valley dialects are rather baffling, and it is easier for a Dane to understand a Swede than vice versa—at any rate it is extremely difficult for a Swede to understand a man from the interior of Jutland. Moreover, we are usually too lazy to read the other countries' books in the original language; they have to be translated—which causes considerable expense, as the reading public in each case is so small. Many individual words sound comic in a neighbouring language: for instance, the Swedish for a butterfly, *fjaril*, becomes in Danish *sommerfugl*, literally 'summer-bird' (incidentally, several German dialects, particularly in the region of Swabia, still call butterflies by the name of *sommervogel*), and *rolig*, which means 'merry' in Swedish, signifies 'quiet' in Danish.

Swedish and Danish are dynamic languages, which have not become set in a classical mould. Only since 1889 has Denmark had an official system of spelling, and that is subjected to periodical revision. The Swedish Academy is far from conservative; it admits current neologisms into its official vocabulary. In the 1930s the plural form of the Swedish verbs was dropped from everyday speech, and in 1945 most of the newspapers decided to adopt this new system.

It was in Norway, however, that the language question took on a really dramatic aspect. In 1380, when Norway was united with Denmark, Danish officials moved into the country and their language was adopted by the administration, the townspeople, the judges and the clergy. To some extent, of course, it was adapted to a Norwegian pronunciation, but it remained a foreign tongue and during the nineteenth century, when Norwegian nationalism was rapidly gathering strength, it came to be regarded with hatred. Bjørnson and Ibsen were the last and greatest writers to use it, and even they realized that if they did not want their writings to be rejected by their countrymen and handed back to Denmark, with or without thanks for the loan, they must thoroughly overhaul their vocabulary. So they changed the spelling as and when they thought fit, introduced dialect words, and gave a Norwegian turn to their phrases wherever possible. But this was only half a solution.

Ivar Aasen (1813–96) was more radical. He sought in remote valleys for the scattered remnants (both fossilized or still evolving) of the independent Norwegian language spoken in ancient times, and in 1852, produced from them his *Landsmål*, an active challenger to the *Riksmål* of Danish origin. In 1882 these two dialects were officially declared equal in status throughout the country. Things did not stop there, however, for every author now felt it incumbent upon him to add something, or make some changes, derived from his own fjord and

II ICELAND

valley. These activities were not confined to the actual vocabulary or to specific points of syntax; for the inner secret of every language lies in its individual rhythm, the way in which it conforms to the mentality of the people. So it is hardly surprising that after three further linguistic reforms, both the Danish-influenced *Bokmål* and the revived, indigenous *Nynorsk* are still bubbling with vitality. The accent, with the rising inflection on the final syllable, sounds as brisk and optimistic as the Norwegian temperament. It will be a long time before the Norwegian language settles into a definitive form. It thus makes a stimulating contrast to Swedish, a firmly consolidated language, characterized in its spoken form by a melodious, slightly sing-song intonation. The Danes speak 'as though their mouths were full of porridge', or so the Swedes declare—though they are frankly envious of the charm and pungency of the Danish tongue.

The Norwegian drama is being re-enacted on the tiny stage of the Faeroes. Here, too, the Danish language finally prevailed over a great number of local dialects, and efforts are now being made to weld these into a standard speech for all the islands. This is a difficult problem—especially as the Faeroes have a wealth of terms used in sheep-breeding, but as yet no words for the achievements of modern civilization. So a creative linguistic system has to be devised for the 32,000 inhabitants of the islands.

Things have been easiest for the Icelanders. On their big island they simply kept to the West Scandinavian dialect of the later Viking Age. So little has it altered that they can still read their seven-hundred-year-old classics in the original—as they are fond of doing.

As well as this there are, of course, two other and completely different languages in Scandinavia—Finnish and Lapp. The four thousand reindeer herdsmen of Lapp descent speak a wide variety of dialects, so that at fairs and in church they are often obliged to resort to the Finnish language—on Swedish territory. As for Finnish, it has borrowed many words from the Swedes, but their pronunciation has been altered beyond recognition. Finnish has no sibilants, no B or P, and few Rs, and its words have only one initial consonant. There is only one gender (*hän* stands for both 'he' and 'she'), but there are fifteen different cases, no prepositions, but a number of 'postpositions' and countless suffixes. With its heavy stress, placed always on the first syllable—many of the words are very long—and its numerous vowel sounds creating an austere harmony, Finnish is an unusually expressive and colourful language; but it is not easy to learn. It received its written form in the sixteenth century, after the Reformation. Finnish was the speech of the settlers who were brought into Sweden to clear patches of forest by fire, but there are few traces left of their language. It is still spoken by the Finnish minorities living along the Torne River, and a Swede from the south will be surprised by occasional bilingual notices and posters in this part of his unified country. On the other hand, the three hundred and fifty thousand Swedes who live in south-west Finland have kept to their own tongue. In spite of all these different languages and dialects, Scandinavian forms a linguistic group, completely distinct from the rest of the European languages, and displaying tremendous vitality and subtle differentiations within itself. Neologisms are still pouring in. Television has recently shown itself to be an effective means of linking the various languages. In the space of ten years it will probably do more to bring the Scandinavian peoples together, from the linguistic standpoint, than the previous century did to drive them apart.

Whenever we speak of Scandinavia as a whole, we look back to the Viking Age, the first creation of a Northern community. It seems as though even nowadays every Scandinavian is a Viking at heart. People see evidence of this in the Nordic peoples' zest for travel, and in their athletic hardiness. They feel that the Scandinavian must be possessed by an original, entirely individual spirit, which may be suppressed for a time, but is always ready to emerge in some new form. Old-fashioned books invariably have the same approach to this subject, no matter to whom they refer. They inform us that the nation concerned—whichever it may be—is proud and self-willed, 'a race set apart'. Some authors describe the Scandinavians as passionate, others declare them to be indolent but quickly roused in the face of danger. They are said to be clean, frugal, persevering, fond of children, trustworthy. So that the panegyric shall not grow too monotonous, the writer then adds a judicious proportion of contrasting characteristics, telling us that the Scandinavians are fond of aping foreigners and have a weakness for their fashions, show some inclination to extravagance and sensuality, and are not always reliable. All this is attributable to the 'thick blood' of the race, and examples are quoted from the dawn of history—which in this case means from the age of the far-travelled Vikings.

All the same it must be remembered that people are the product of their environment. The way of life of a nation is conditioned by its education, its economic circumstances and its spiritual standards. There is no such thing as a national 'soul' or a nation-wide ability in any particular direction. Intelligence, temperament, impulses and inclinations vary with the individual, and are to a great extent shaped by environment. It would thus be incorrect to maintain that the Viking spirit is a racial characteristic of the Scandinavian peoples, though it does, of course, form part of their common heritage. The formative influence of their natural surroundings, their unchanging forests and wave-splashed coasts, is still at work too, as we shall see when we come to consider each nation individually.

The Danes were perhaps in the best position to preserve their Viking heritage through the Christian Middle Ages. The free, land-owning farmer-warriors banded together in a voluntary levy to defend their shores against the Hansa and the Wends. They were impatient of the growing influence exerted by the consolidated central administration of the country. For instance, they warned the Kings and the Archbishops, who were working hand-in-glove, that 'To proceed against the People with thunder and lightning is regarded as a great offence on the part of the King, and one not to be left unpunished, for which reason the people, meeting in the "Thing", at once repealed all the royal taxes, refused to pay tithes to the Bishops, and granted the clergy the right to marry. . . . The people declared that the clergy were able to conduct the church services by themselves, and that Bishops were therefore no longer needed.' (*Saxo Grammaticus.*)

But Denmark, as a rising international power, did need a force of cavalry, and the feudal lords could meet the high cost of providing mounted soldiers only if they were relieved from the burden of taxation. In the reign of Valdemar II Sejr (1202–41) a privileged aristocracy came into existence, its members individually taking the oath of allegiance to the King. Valdemar Atterdag (1340–75) even recruited military commanders from Holstein to take charge of his castles. This is how the families of Moltke and Ahlefeldt, to mention only two names, first came to Denmark.

Few peasants did well enough to have any prospect of joining the equestrian order. They had to become the tenant-farmers of the new overlords. By about 1350 a great proportion of the peasants had lost their freedom. Denmark had become a feudal State after the Central European pattern. Matters gradually reached a point at which peasant families were compelled to remain in the same farm for generations, unless the overlord decided to sell his serfs! They also had to work for their lord (*Hoveri*) whenever he chose to demand it. In 1700, when these forms of bondage were brought to an end, the great ones of the land protested furiously, for it was their duty to provide soldiers to fight in the perpetual wars. As a result, the year 1733 saw the promulgation of an equally unpopular decree (*Stavnsbåndet*), by which no peasant might leave his birthplace between the ages of four and forty. With such a social system, it is not surprising that the Danes gradually lost their fighting spirit.

Ludvig Holberg (1684–1754) has left us a picture of the coast-dwelling *Husmand* in all his cheerless abasement. 'Jeppe på Bjerget' describes his own case:

'The village folk say Jeppe drinks, but they do not say why Jeppe drinks.' He does it because his wife beats him to try to induce him to be of some help about the house. Then the estate bailiff beats him to try to induce him to work for the landlord. And finally the village organist makes a cuckold of him and jeers at him into the bargain because he takes it without protest. Now why does Jeppe not hit back? In the first place because he is afraid, in the second place because his wife wears the breeches, and in the third place because, as he says himself, 'Jeppe is a kindhearted fellow and a good Christian, who never seeks revenge'. It is true that one day when, after getting extremely drunk, Jeppe wakes to find himself in the Baron's bed, he does try, from this unexpected position of authority, to avenge himself on the little local officials. But Holberg ends by concluding that the reins of power ought not to be placed in hands that were meant to guide the plough. What wonder that eighteenth-century Denmark produced no folk poetry and displayed little affection for hearth and home? But an awakening was to come.

N. F. S. Grundtvig (1783–1872) was a divine, a romantic poet, and an enthusiastic student of the ancient Nordic religion. He 'read about the old days in a clear, serene voice; with lively pleasure traced the Saviour's life through the writings of the Church. Oh, what would become of us, were we to forget that holy, happy time!' In his sermons, Grundtvig proclaimed a radiant, cheerful Christianity with nothing gruesome or tragic about it and without the fateful 'conversion' that was a prominent feature of many sects. A place in the Christian community was everyone's birthright, he declared. Baptism, Communion and the Creed were important stages on the path by which the individual gradually gained full membership of the community of the faithful, with the tranquillity it brings. The new Danish way of life becomes easier to understand if we realize that Grundtvig had manic-depressive tendencies. Four times in the course of his life he was treated for nervous depression. During the intervening periods his preaching had a power of persuasion that amounted to genius.

His simple words, with their direct appeal, were addressed to the Danish *Husmand* and peasant, who spent his monotonous days trudging behind his oxen, with no eyes or ears for anything else. He too was to have his share of the good things of the earth, sunshine and bird-song, munificent harvests, cattle and flowers, leisure and enjoyment.

This, of course, also entailed some practical economic reforms, particularly land clearance and social emancipation. The large farms were expropriated by law; the hungry and destitute received State loans with which to buy land for themselves. Present-day Denmark is proud of its great number of prosperous farming families, and small farms receive more encouragement than in any other country.

From now on the country population, too, was to receive a modern education. Grundtvig's cheerful words appealed directly to the emotions. He wanted to rouse his listeners, to hold them and entertain them. *Det levende Ord*—the living Word—so he called his message. Its form was forthright and personal, its content rich in picturesque touches, humour and irony and first-hand observation. By its very nature it lacked spiritual depth and gravity, but the young audiences in Denmark's 'People's Universities' gladly surrendered to its appeal to their spirit and intellect; it roused them to a sense of their surroundings, even if their attention was apt to be concentrated on trivialities. It can hardly have been by accident that the first of these People's Universities, opened in 1844, was at Rödding, just north of the frontier between Germany and Denmark—where it provided spiritual reinforcement for the Danes in Sönderjylland.

Denmark's decline from the position of a great Power contributed to this cultural revival in more ways than one. The country had suffered many severe blows in rapid succession. In 1801, it had been obliged to accept England's conditions, in 1807 the English had bombarded Copenhagen, in 1814 Norway had been lost, and from 1814 to 1830 there were a number of agricultural and industrial crises; the conclusion of the war against Prussia in 1848, though not decisive, was dispiriting, and finally, in 1864, came the loss of Sönderjylland.

This series of defeats was too much—more especially as people could still remember the old, proud days when Skåne, Blekinge, Halland, Estonia, the island of Gotland in the Baltic and several areas on the northern coast of Germany had belonged to Denmark.

It is not surprising that a nation should alter its way of life under the impression of such events. The Danes turned their backs on glory, power and might, deciding they were not worth while. The triumph of individualism and of a new inwardness found expression in the writings of Søren Kierkegaard. Grundtvig's advocacy of the well-filled, happy, simple life and his emphasis on individual psychological observation appealed not only to the peasants, as something they could understand, but became equally popular with the country's cultural *élite*. Heart and mind united to erect these ideas as the standard by which everything should be measured. Henceforth the goal was not to be absolute power, but the cultivation of those hidden treasures which are the real, genuine things in life.

Hans Christian Andersen, the writer of fairy-tales, told the story of the Emperor's new clothes. Everyone praised their magnificence, until a little unsophisticated boy exclaimed, 'But he has nothing on at all!' Another of Andersen's tales is about the Ugly Duckling—also meant as a reference to himself. Everyone persecutes the Ugly Duckling and jeers at him—until spring comes and he turns into a big, beautiful swan. 'It does no harm to be born in a poultry-yard, provided you come out of a swan's egg.'

The Danes combine remarkable modesty with a firm belief that only those hidden, inner, and entirely personal values are worth striving for; they are thus just as self-confident as other nations—but in their own way.

This spirit of confident modesty also indicates the standard by which we must be guided if we are to come to terms with Denmark and particularly with Copenhagen. The visitor to that city finds that it includes an old district in a good state of preservation and a few buildings, marked by their greenish copper roofs and turrets, dating from Denmark's period as a great Power. But the present-day traveller, surfeited by the vast number of historical monuments he has seen elsewhere, expects a capital to offer him something unique and unparalleled; so he wanders hesitantly up and down the streets of Copenhagen. Radhuspladsen is, of course, the centre of the town, but it has no striking, monumental architecture. Then there is Ströget, the famous old street reserved for pedestrians. This is narrow, so that its house-fronts, not in themselves impressive, are difficult to take in at a glance, and its shop-windows are crowded to their utmost capacity with goods and price-tickets. The eye is never drawn towards one particular example of the latest fashion; it has to inspect each dress laboriously before deciding what it finds attractive. Nor do the girls and young women make an impression of elegance; sometimes they seem positively careless of their appearance. But some glimpse of their hidden quality may be caught from a vivacious glance, a terse, rapid phrase, or the special Danish smile, *det danske smil*.

Visiting the popular National Museum, we see stone hatchets, amber necklaces, bronze axe-heads, iron swords and gold ornaments crowded together like the goods in the shop windows, and wonder where, amid this profusion, certain unique treasures are to be found. The visitor is expected to gain added pleasure from seeking and discovering them for himself.

Where else in the world could there be a genuinely popular 'Tivoli' like the one at Copenhagen? There the Changing of the Guard is carried out by a boys' band playing lustily, its members wearing the same eighteenth-century uniform as the grown-up soldiers in front of the Royal Palace. The Danes themselves find the performance just as delightfully comic as it seems to foreign visitors. The old figures of the Commedia dell'Arte have found a refuge in the Tivoli, and the gardens have plenty of quiet nooks to reward those who take the trouble to explore.

Where else would one find the harbour—Nyhavn—close beside the Royal Palace? The atmosphere there is not of the most decorous; but the Danes' sense of humour—which has been a thorn in the side of so many Swedes at various times—is irresistibly tickled by the solemnity with which their thirsty neighbours come streaming across the Öresjön for a drink. At one time the Copenhagen police had to open a special 'Swedish prison', where these guests from over the water could sleep off their potations and, if necessary, be fitted out with new clothes.

In those days Storm P. became the typical Danish humorist:

'Tell me, Storm P., why do you always draw Swedes with red noses?'

'Ho-ho—how else would people know they were Swedes?'

Even nowadays one sees a remarkable number of old cars in Denmark. This is due, of course, to the very high purchase-tax on new cars, but there is something typical in the affectionate care with which Ford T Models and other private cars of the 1930s are kept spick and span. There are many charming colour-schemes, amusing accessories, and chintz-curtained windows. The Danes are not impressed by outsized cars and yards of chromium plating. And throughout the country one sees evidence of a similar attitude in other walks of life—not only in the small businesses and trim farmhouses, but also in the desire to give fair treatment to the national minorities—the Germans and Eskimos—and ensure freedom of opinion for everyone.

The hardest blow came with the Occupation, on 9 April 1940. It was virtually impossible for the Danes to offer any direct resistance to force. They had to surrender almost without a struggle. That day, King Christian X did not ride alone through the streets of his capital, as was his custom; but he did so on 10 April. This was neither an acceptance of what had happened, nor an attempt to diminish its importance. It was an observance of a typically Danish custom, a silent appeal to the nation to remain true to itself. That was perhaps most difficult of all after 1945—to refrain from making any territorial claim on South Schleswig, to tolerate the reappearance of a German minority party in Parliament (recognition has now been given to the Danish minority in the Kiel Parliament as a measure of reciprocity), and to resume co-operation with Denmark's southern neighbour.

The last thousand years of Danish history thus fall into three sections, marked by three clearly differentiated ways of life. They show how completely a nation is the product of the prevailing social, economic and spiritual circumstances. Those circumstances may be ephemeral or lasting; in either case they are created by the mind of man. The special Danish attitude towards life becomes even clearer and more significant when we consider it in relation to that of the other Scandinavian countries.

Norway, too, carried its Viking traditions into the Christian Middle Ages, but its destiny was very different. After enjoying a succession of vigorous independent rulers, Norway concluded a union with the Swedish royal house in 1319, and in 1380 with that of Denmark. For the next 434 years the Norwegians were subject to the Danes, with no voice in their own government.

Here we must take another look at the structure of the country. It had a peasant population, dwelling in isolated log-houses along the fjords, or in the valleys running through the wild mountain landscape. The people paid little attention even to the local priest; in any case he usually lived a long way off. They mingled the heathen customs of their ancestors with the rites of the Church to which, as Christians, they now owed obedience. They worked out their beliefs, each for himself, as best they could. Pagan statues were still to be seen in some farmyards as late as the eighteenth century and at that period many a farmer could tell the parson proudly in which barrow his heathen forebears lay buried. Attention was entirely taken up by local problems. As a modern writer puts it: 'At one time we used to have a lot of trouble with the ford across the river. But later on it was paved and made firm. That was in King Öystein's reign.' Öystein died in 1123! In the circumstances, it made little difference whether the King was ruling from Oslo or from Copenhagen. The new civic sense that arose in the Middle Ages had no real chance to develop. Every administrative measure, every attempt to establish connections, petered out among the beetling crags and desolate mountain wastes. The tax-collectors arrived with their demands. These were submitted to, just as, for general purposes, the authority of the Norwegian State was recognized, but the local crops and the fishing catch were more important. A man might visit the nearest town, where he would see the Danish

IV   DENMARK, THE NYHAVN

officials, perhaps have dealings with them. But then he would go back to his valley, where foreigners hardly ever set foot. What scope was there for building castles? Norway itself was one huge rock-fortress. No aristocracy could come into existence there, and no standing army.

It was really the travelling merchants who had the chief say in the country's affairs. A ship used to sail from Bergen to Greenland every summer, but unfortunately it sank in 1367. There was a considerable trade in dried fish, blubber and hides, which were exported to England and Germany. The Hanseatic merchants carried them further south. A relic of this trade is to be seen in the 'Tyske Bryggen' at Bergen, with its merchants' quarters and warehouses; unfortunately it has recently been badly damaged by a fire which broke out in its dry timbers.

In the eighteenth century the flourishing trade with England and the Norwegian seafaring activities expanded rapidly. The country came into closer contact with the outside world, and the ancient peasant culture gradually awoke from its slumber. Students were no longer obliged to go to Copenhagen University—in 1811 they were given one of their own, at Christiania.

Events moved rapidly after this. Karl Johan Bernadotte, the heir to the Swedish throne, ostensibly on his way to France, wheeled round and threatened Denmark instead. By the terms of the peace treaty signed at Kiel in January 1814, Norway passed to him. But the Norwegians, taking matters into their own hands, convened an impromptu Parliament at Eidsvold in May of that year, and proclaimed their independence. Karl Johan turned his forces against Norway, but finally agreed to a compromise by which he acknowledged the new Norwegian Constitution, but imposed a union with Sweden. This settlement was upheld by the Congress of Vienna and the Norwegians decided to rest on their laurels.

However, their sense of nationalism was now awakened. As we have already seen, they discovered the scenic beauty of their country and built up a Norwegian language; collectors and scholars assembled the long-neglected treasures of the past and invoked the proud history of the period of independence; Grieg emerged as the greatest of the strictly Norwegian composers, and national writers were actively at work. Ibsen's *Peer Gynt* was offset by the stern, inflexible *Brand*, less familiar only because the play defeats all attempts at stage production. Both figures represent aspects of humanity, and aspects which are especially characteristic of Norway.

Bjørnstjerne Bjørnson composed the bright national anthem, *'Ja vi elsker dette landet . . .'*, and everybody wanted to join in singing it. The next objective of the rapidly developing Norwegian nationalism was an independent foreign policy—in short, a complete end to the union with Sweden. In 1905 the situation became acute. King Oskar II gave way, and the Norwegians held a plebiscite—by which they elected the brother of the Danish King as their own ruler, and he came to the throne as Håkon VII. So the old breach with Denmark was bridged after all, and Scandinavian unity suffered no real setback in 1905. It was appreciated that any voluntary and sincere association must be based upon respect for the wishes and rights of all the partners.

At this point the Norwegians abolished the Danish name of their capital—'Christiania' was rechristened 'Oslo'. In point of fact the site of the original Oslo had been in the vicinity of Ekeberg, but it was destroyed by fire in 1624 and the modern city grew up beside the fortress of Akershus. Most of it dates from the nineteenth and twentieth centuries. This combination of hoary antiquity with a vigorous activity sponsored by the newborn nationalist sentiment is to be encountered all over the country.

Oslo has *one* important street, named after Karl Johan. It climbs uphill to the Royal Palace, which is a replica of the 'Carolina' at Uppsala, but with an extra balcony, in the purest Empire style. The residential and commercial streets are centred on this, with no attempt at self-contained planning.

The buildings—the Town Hall, the Post Office and so forth—are ponderous and angular; it seems as though great rocks had been dragged into the city and deposited there. Dictators are fond of erecting gigantic buildings as an advertisement for their own power. But it is a quite different thing for a democratic nation to aim at a monumental effect, especially in a country which is not wealthy. Yet this is the impression made by Oslo on visitors coming from the other Scandinavian countries—for example, at the sight of Per Krogh's frescoes and glass-paintings in the University library, which embrace the walls and windows in a single bold sweep. Where except in Norway do we find an open-air display of sculpture like that of the Gustav Vigeland Park? Its effect is not due entirely to the individual works—the *Foetus*, the *Phallus*, the entwined couples—the imposing dignity of the general plan also contributes to it, with the steps leading up to the dominant monolith, and the empty pediments awaiting other statues. In fact the design is frankly too ambitious for its purpose and for the local possibilities.

Compare it with Oslo's other open-air museum—Bygdøy. Only in Norway have well-preserved Viking ships come to light so far (those found off the coast of Schleswig and in Roskilde fjord are fragmentary wreckage). Yet Norway has three of them—the Tune ship, King Olav Geirstada-Alf's Gokstad ship and Queen Åsa's ship from Oseberg. It was in these open vessels that the Vikings discovered and colonized Iceland, Greenland and the continent of America and conquered England. Not only has present-day Norway regained something of the adventurous zest that marked that epoch; it has some tangible relics of it to show as well. At a later period, stave churches were built, with the same stout timbers as the old ships. One example, from Gol, has been brought to Bydgøy; others, such as those at Urnes, Borgund and Heddal, still stand among their meadows, with life going on happily around them. They are tiny buildings, but they thrust valiantly upwards, as though seeking to rival the frowning cliffs. Some have porches decorated by the earliest Viking converts to Christianity with carvings of knots and dragons. Wood is supposed to be a perishable material, unsuitable for the creation of enduring monuments. Yet the Viking ships buried in the earth and the stave churches standing on its firm surface have survived for nine hundred or a thousand years to impress modern men with their bold lines.

That is Norway's eternal problem—how to come to terms with the mighty features of a landscape too vast to be shaped by human hands. Its inhabitants could be content for centuries with their peasant life, but they could never develop the idyllic sensitiveness of the Danes. And now, raised to greater stature by their national feeling, they have to grapple with their perpetual problem once more. Their Occupation during the Second World War was more bitterly felt by the Norwegians; they suffered it in silence, and for that reason their wounds, being of a spiritual nature, take longer to heal than those of other people. That is something we must respect.

Besides, they have never learnt to work together in numbers in a small area. They are more inclined to withdraw, each in his own direction. They know, as we all do, that the nineteenth-century type of nationalism has vanished for ever. With it has gone the mainspring of the enthusiasm that spurred them to fresh achievements; but since 1814 they have lived too much to themselves to be able to surrender easily to other trends. Democracy is the perfectly natural order of things for them; in the nineteenth century everyone in the country lived on exactly the same footing. A constructive future undoubtedly awaits Norway. The nation's recent surge of resilience, eager and dramatic, will find fresh means of expression within the existing social and economic framework.

The third of these brother nations, with the same Viking traditions as its heritage, again followed a completely different path. It is this variety that gives Scandinavia its fascination. Sweden developed a firm central administration, but without the totalitarian aspects of the Danish system; here the peasants and the rest of the population never lost their freedom. To put it the other way round, the self-confident peasants were able to hold their own in this spacious, thinly-populated land as well as in Norway, but natural conditions were not such as to prevent the King from being an effective ruler. Even during the long winter, all parts of the country could be reached comparatively quickly on skis or sledges; in summer, ships could sail along the coast and up the rivers to the lakes, maintaining communication with the interior. Thus, a clergyman once set out from Stockholm after his Sunday service to travel to Lund (390 miles) and back, and appeared punctually in his pulpit again the following Sunday. King Karl XI used to mount his couriers on elks—an animal which had apparently been ridden in Finland from time immemorial. In this way they reached the greatest speeds known to man before the technical age, covering as much as 200 miles a day and carrying reports of the movement of hostile armies more rapidly than anyone else could do. They must have been a magnificent sight, these swift riders on their huge, antlered, prehistoric steeds, outstripping all other travellers.

The open landscape offered the King the technical facilities for ruling—but not the power. In every feudal State, the monarch had to rely on an aristocracy, a privileged class, to strengthen his position. In Sweden, however, there was no basis for the existence of such people; there was not a single peak on which a castle could be erected, not a single river whose fords could be easily controlled. Even the profits to be made by clearing and cultivating a patch of forest were often too scanty to tempt ambition. So, in complete contrast to the position in Denmark, we find the knights continuing to live among the peasant communities. Many of them were perfectly content to take up farming again, once they realized there was no advantage to be earned in the King's service. So the knightly order was in the last resort a question of economic necessity, with no idealistic aspirations attaching to it, and that sober, practical attitude seems to have survived down to modern times in what was never a rich country.

A few land-owners built up great estates and thus needed tenants, but in this cold region the harvest was so uncertain that everyone was obliged to help his neighbour, without distinction between landlord and tenant farmer. A knight's estates would be scattered all over the country, so the nobility had no chance to build up a territorial domination—only in the service

20

V DENMARK

of the State could power and influence be acquired. And the Swedish 'Imperial Council', in its dealings with the King, was perhaps more representative of the nation as a whole than the corresponding body in any other country.

Thus there arose a democratically controlled administrative system which, by the way, is the second oldest in Europe. Only the Merovingian kingdom preceded it—and France has long ceased to be a monarchy. The first powerful Kings of the Svear are buried in the three royal tumuli at Uppsala and in various other mounds of equal size. In the sixth and seventh centuries the Ynglingar dynasty defeated a number of neighbouring petty kings and gained an unquestionable influence over the Gotar, further to the south of Sweden. They wished to commemorate these successes by the vast proportions of their burial places.

The present administrative structure of Sweden is firmly and confidently rooted in the historical continuity which has always been a support to the rulers and their people alike. The peasants drove out King Erik of Pomerania, King Karl Knutsson Bonde (though his last name means 'peasant'!) and King Christian II of Denmark. They never allowed King Gustav Vasa to forget that he owed his throne to their goodwill. They formed one of the four parties in the parliament at a time when the Danish peasants were serfs and Norway had no parliament at all.

On the other hand, the Swedish peasants were always prepared to co-operate with a reasonable King. The taxes, having been voted by the people through their representatives, must be accepted patiently and paid. They had passed the laws, and so they obeyed them. They chose their own clergy. Nominees were, and still are, required to demonstrate their ability by delivering sample sermons and, once in position, they would be called to order by the community if it seemed necessary. The central government was not permitted to interfere in any aspect of local affairs. Even such offences as assault or robbery, and measures such as the enforcement of maintenance orders, were never submitted in the first place to the *Thing*, or district court; the peasants settled these matters among themselves. At present the small country communities are being amalgamated into larger units, and this calls for the careful adaptation of local government regulations to meet the new circumstances.

All this explains the extreme punctiliousness of the Swedes, which contrasts so strongly with the Danes' friendly, courteous charm of manner and the impetuous enthusiasm of the individualistic Norwegians. The strict formalism that characterizes Swedish public business is something quite different from the bureaucratic red tape by which most countries are irritated nowadays. The foreigner visiting Sweden is apt to feel stifled by this love of organization; however much he finds in the country to admire, this remains irksome. Without a knowledge of the historical background, it can hardly be otherwise. For the Swedes themselves it is perfectly natural, however, and most of them are quite unconscious of anything unusual in their behaviour.

Carefully, they paint yellow lines along the roads, to sort the cars into parallel lanes. Every car must keep to its own *Fil*. Any driver who changes his *Fil* is frowned upon by the others and severely criticized. Horns toot a warning to anyone who exceeds the speed-limit. Driving in Stockholm has thus become a highly skilled social exercise. The more complicated the rules, the more satisfaction people feel, for it shows that justice is being enforced in the traffic system.

A maximum of social justice is also striven for in the wage system, health insurance, old age pensions and the new primary schools. Stockholm is rapidly expanding; new blocks of flats and offices are springing up like mushrooms (over 14,000 new homes per year). But the growth of the population is too rapid even so, and young married couples anxious for a home of their own have to wait, nowadays, for an average of more than four years. People wait patiently for their turn to move into one of the new houses, which are so uniform, inside and out. This has long ceased to be a sign of conformity and is accepted as a necessary adaptation to circumstances in which nobody must have grounds for complaint or receive preferential treatment.

Stockholm has none of the reticent charm of Copenhagen, which waits to be discovered; nor does it emulate Oslo's strenuous efforts to achieve massive dignity. Stockholm's ambition is to be modern and smart. Whatever is reported from anywhere in the world as the latest thing, Stockholm must have it too. The whole place is being pulled down—no great loss in itself— and replanned more drastically than any bombed-out city in Europe. It already has five sky-scrapers, twenty storeys high and with three more floors underground. Here we find a cheerful, winding shopping street, reserved for pedestrians; elsewhere there is a traffic roundabout that deals with a hundred thousand cars a day; in the centre of this is a restaurant with a fountain playing on its glass roof. More cars rush through subterranean tunnels and the first through-trains on the underground are already in operation.

Stockholm certainly makes the most of its third dimension; traffic dives into the ground or comes tearing out of it; people drive down a steep slope to a garage lying far beneath a church, come up from it again in the lift, are carried to a height of over 100 feet by the Katharina chair lift, or stroll about in a restaurant that hangs in mid-air. Building plans have been completed up to the year 1970. The solutions to the various problems are so original that every month brings fresh amazement—original, but perhaps characteristic of Sweden. Who can say, as yet? These new concrete buildings show no sign of a feeling for history. But their soaring, uncluttered lines are bracing as the Nordic air, vigorous and rapid as our own period, smart and elegant as every Swede likes to imagine himself.

Because at the bottom of their hearts the Swedes are not really interested in what is 'foreign', they can accept 'foreign' things uncritically and without reservations. This may sound para-doxical, but it is really quite simple. The Swede makes a point of spending his holidays in Germany, England, France, the Alps or the Mediterranean, not only because he can afford to, but because he really thinks it worth while and wants to see something different. Then, deeply impressed, he returns home—to his black bread and herring. He will adopt the most ridiculous American crazes, whereas the Danes, with their ironical sense of humour, and the Norwegians, with their self-respect, would never dream of doing so. It pleases him but has no real importance for him. He never feels that his personality may be influenced; whatever happens he will remain typically Swedish.

The sense of a 'greater Sweden' is, strange as it may seem, on occasion expressed very readily by the seven-and-a-half million members of this nation. True, the concept is difficult to define; it is prompted not so much by nationalist feeling as by a kind of self-confidence: 'We used to be a fine lot, and . . . Nils Andersson is very "greater Sweden" in his way, there's no denying that'. What has this Nils Andersson done? Perhaps he celebrated his fiftieth birthday by a substantial contribution to some cause *and* a big party—doing things in style. This kind of thing should be noticed, but without ostentation: 'Well, you see, I thought somebody ought to do something about it. And as it so happened, I had the money to spare just then. It's not worth talking about. When do you and your family leave for Sicily, old man?'

No Swede can resist the challenge of the rising standard of living; better clothes, housing and food are demanded as a natural right. But luxuries, too, easily come to be regarded as necessities, and few people can grasp the fact that it is possible to have other interests and therefore be reluctant to join in the dazzling rat-race. The Swede is only too ready to assume that what is large is also grand, and psychological insight is not his strong point. That is why he falls such an easy prey to the subtle mockery of the Danes and why he delights so much in the inimitable charms of French culture.

But Sweden, like Denmark, was once a great Power, and saw the collapse of that greatness. Surely that must have left its mark here too? In 1718, Sweden lost most of its provinces on the far side of the Baltic and in 1809 even Finland slipped away. Dire poverty, loss of population and values—the nation may have been obliged to repress considerable aggressiveness at this period. It is conceivable that this is how the reputed coldness of the Swedes originated. The Norwegian capacity for enthusiasm finds no echo here. That may be the explanation of the Swede's emotional sluggishness and his lack of interest in psychology. But this is by no means certain, for in 1718 Sweden came into permanent possession of the three formerly Danish provinces, and in 1814 came the compensation of union with Norway. Sweden's period as a great Power had lasted only eighty-eight years in all and the political decline was less marked than Denmark's.

The Finns played no active part in the Viking Age. Their language is not of Germanic origin. Nevertheless, they are a Scandinavian people.

The Finns moved into their present territory in prehistoric times, coming from the south-east. For many centuries they lived the uneventful life of hunters and fishers, clearing patches of the vast forests by fire and cultivating them, moving on after a few harvests to clear a new patch. These primitive customs remained with them down to modern times.

Swedish merchants settled along the Gulf of Bothnia during the Viking period. Their graves have been opened and found to contain examples of the goods they obtained through barter, in exchange for furs from the forests of Finland. Swedish farmers settled on the coast, retaining the habits, speech and style of building they had brought from their western homeland. King Erik the Saint is reputed to have led a crusade to Finland before 1160, and a hundred years later the country was a recognized part of the Swedish domains.

It would never have occurred to anyone that the Finns should not become Swedish subjects, merely because they differed in language, origin and economic system. They were the boldest and most trusty riders 'on Narva's moorlands, Poland's sands, on Leipzig's plain or Lützen's hill', as Runeberg wrote in a Finnish March; they were in the van of the Swedish army in the fiercest battles.

The growth of nationalism divided the peoples and bred hatred among them for the first

VI SWEDEN

time; but it also strengthened the self-confidence of the millions in Europe and throughout the world. At the dawn of the nineteenth century, the Finns had nothing they could call their own. Unlike the Norwegians, they had no long-vanished political liberties to look back upon, no heroic period of bardic legend. The disastrous war of 1808–9 divided them from Sweden and brought them under Russian rule. At that time the Tsarist censorship was extremely severe, there could be no question of political controversy in the newspapers; the country came under bureaucratic dictatorship; it was feared that the University of Åbo would be arbitrarily moved to St Petersburg and Finland incorporated into the Slav empire in every respect. Swedish remained the only language used in learned circles and in the law-courts.

Amid this intellectual torpor a new note began to be heard: 'We are no longer Swedes, we do not wish to become Russians, we must be Finns.' The situation is revealed by a document dating from 1847, which bears the signatures of eleven young Academicians. It declares, among other things, that anyone who does not yet know the Finnish language should hasten to learn it, that people should whenever possible avoid speaking Swedish among themselves, and that the sacred interests of the Fatherland and the Mother-tongue can be promoted only if a love for them can be aroused in the hearts of the young, who are perhaps still uncorrupted.

Meanwhile there had already been developments. In 1835 *Kalevala* had appeared. Elias Lönnrot had gone far afield, into the forests, visiting huts, cottages and log-houses, and had collected one-and-a-half million stanzas of Finnish folk poetry. These he compared and, selecting the best and most complete versions, welded them into the form of a continuous epic. He added a thousand lines of his own to hold the poem together, altered or added names and ideas, and finally published this 'mosaic' of 22,795 lines. It comprehends the entire life of Finland. It gives glimpses of a primitive heroic poetry, into which a number of fairy-tales had been absorbed as the centuries went by. Some of its themes probably go back as far as the migration of the nations; it is peopled with magicians and nature plays a more vital part in life here than in any other body of folk poetry.

It tells of Ilmarinen, the smith of the gods, who, when the world was created, hammered out the vault of heaven so skilfully that 'no mark of the hammer is to be seen, no man can see where the pincers gripped'. Old, wise Väinämöinen, a Wotan-like figure, sings his magic verses to defeat Joukahainen: 'Lake waters rage, the earth heaves, copper mountains tremble, hard rocks of slate fall asunder, primeval mountains dash to pieces, the cliffs of the sea are rent apart. . . . He sings Joukahainen up to the hips in the bog, sings him up to the chin in mud.'

Then there is handsome Kaukomieli, a jaunty, fickle youth. Cheerfully, he lies with every virtuous maiden at Saari: 'He puts an end to the virgin's laughter, he silences the tittering girl, he lays a child in the arms of them all'. So mockery of him ceases, and he proudly wins the hand of Kylliki, the noble virgin, the flower of Saari. There are fierce sea-fights with Pohja's people—archers, warriors with their broad-swords, war-ships. But the Finns love their land: 'May we ever live happy, may we die with honour on the beauteous shores of Suomi, in lovely Karelia!'

Three years after the *Kalevala* epic came Johan Ludvig Runeberg's *Ensign Stål's Stories*—a glorification of Finnish heroism in the war of 1808–9, written in Swedish but adopted forth-with by the whole Finnish people. 'How much stronger than ever before was the sense of belonging to a people among whom life is worth living!'

All this inevitably led to clashes with the Swedish community in the country. Its members spoke Swedish, they were highly educated, their hotels were known as *Societetshus*, to stress their lasting aloofness from all that was purely Finnish. On the other hand, all Finland's cultural leanings were towards Sweden, Sweden had always been ready to help in time of need, relations with Sweden were close and good. The dual tendency is unique and always perceptible: the Swedish language was being gradually ousted from Finland as the Finns waged their national battle against 'foreign' minorities, but then there were those firm bonds of friendship. Finland needed Sweden, and vice versa. Both were part of Scandinavia.

The same mingling of attraction and antipathy is revealed in the national character. The Swedes of Sweden and the Swedish community in Finland have the same ancient culture and are more extrovert and resilient, whereas the Finns are reserved, more serious, slower to react, but given to sudden bursts of rage or enthusiasm. The Swedes, being closest to them, feel this most strongly—this active quiescence of the Finns which brings everyone under their spell. Having no period of national power to look back upon, the Finns reveal true inward greatness in their kinship with nature. Fate dealt them their fair share of hard blows during the nineteenth and twentieth centuries. They invariably met these with a discipline which proved too strong for the nervous, mercurial temperament of their enemies.

All north Scandinavians are individualists, but they show it in different ways—the Norwegians in their austere enthusiasms, the Swedes in their practicality, the Finns in their self-command. Finland is a country of small houses scattered in lonely places over the wide, stern landscape. The people who live there may have no more than a weekly bus to link them with the outer world, where, however, their national peculiarities can find freer expression than those of other peoples. They reveal an inner, creative ability in everything they undertake—hence the staying-power they display in athletics and forest work, their sometimes almost shocking hardness, and the unqualified respect with which all their neighbours regard them.

In Helsinki, the 'white city', capital of Finland, the many neo-Classical buildings include an Olympic stadium and houses designed by Väinö Aaltonen and others; it has become famous as a centre of modern architecture. Power stations and factories with every modern perfection are going up. But the country, in comparison with others, is very poor. The limitations thus imposed would be more evident were it not for the concentrated yet restrained intensity of feeling which can be sensed in every department of life. This brings victory over the poor soil of the country, and victory expressed even in renunciation; it produces the note of triumph in Sibelius's *Finlandia* and that pensive, yet coruscating fancy which, first appearing in the folk art, finds full expression in the modern poets and artists, and can be sensed even in the language with its increasing sprightliness of tone.

A certain Gardarr Svarvarsson was a typically cosmopolitan figure of the Viking Age. He was a Swede by birth, owned a farm on the Danish island of Zealand and was married to a Norwegian woman. He set out for the Hebrides to take up an inheritance but, driven off his course by a storm near the Orkneys, sailed far till one day he made landfall. He sailed round the coast, discovered it to be a large island and gave it his own name—Gardarholm.

At about the same time—this was in the 860s—a Norwegian called Naddodr was washed ashore on the same island. He climbed a high mountain, from which he saw that the country was uninhabited. He returned to his ship and sailed southwards to his home, where he reported his discovery of the island, calling it 'Snowland'.

Floki Vilgerdarson, of west Norway, liked the idea of the island. He sailed away to visit it, taking cattle with him in his ship. He found it was plentifully supplied with fish and birds' eggs, but he did not trouble to collect hay for his cattle and when winter came they starved to death. He lost a ship as well. The spring proved very cold, and when he looked northwards from the mountains he saw a great many ice-floes. Ill-humour prompted him to name the country 'Iceland'.

It is an island full of sharp contrasts—geysers and glaciers, lush meadowland and arid mountains, long, light hours in summer and perpetual darkness in winter, for it lies close to the Arctic circle. The very land for proud farmers who would not submit to the domination of King Harald Fairhair (Haraldr inn Hárfagri), resenting not so much the comparatively light taxation he tried to impose upon them as the idea of surrendering even a modicum of their independence. Such were the men who left Norway between 874 and 930, at the time when the country was being unified. By far the greater number of them flocked across to Iceland, where they established a kindred community of independent farmers. The first-comers could take as much land as they wanted and they settled on the south and west coasts, which are washed by the Gulf Stream. Later arrivals had to make do with the north and east coasts, which are washed by the Arctic current. The names of a thousand men appear in the book of settlements (*Landnámabók*). By about 930 the population had increased to nearly twenty thousand. From the cultural and economic standpoints, the thirteenth century—the period of the sagas—was Iceland's heyday.

Then came the decline—long periods of famine, stagnation, political subjection to Norway and Denmark.

Now Iceland is an independent Republic again, with the proud claim to the oldest democratic legislative assembly in the world; for in 1930 the *Althing* celebrated the thousandth anniversary of its foundation. The country is thriving, with a prosperous economy, and has a population of 170,000.

The Icelanders feel a personal and cultural relationship with the other Scandinavians. Indeed, they claim to be the most genuine descendants of the Vikings, whose manuscripts they can still read in the original. Even today, Haldor Laxness and other Icelandic writers look upon life with a psychological rigour and lucidity which the rest of the Scandinavians have lost.

About the year 900, a would-be settler on his way to Iceland was blown westward off his course, and sighted a group of islands. But not until 982 were these explored—by Erik the Red, who set out again four years later, with twenty-five ships and about six hundred people, to colonize the big island he called Greenland. The fleet ran into storms, and only half the ships reached their goal. The survivors settled round Eystribygd and Vestibygd, on the west coast, where they established a free peasant republic on the Icelandic model. At one time the population may have risen to over three thousand. There was always a suggestion of the Arctic

VII   STOCKHOLM, THE ORPHEUS FOUNTAIN

about life here, along the narrow green strip that edged the fjords, at the foot of gigantic mountains and in the vicinity of the inland ice. From October to May there was no communication with the world outside, and people felt the lack of many things regarded in their homeland as necessities, particularly corn, iron and wood. Iron, however, could be shipped over regularly from Iceland and driftwood could be utilized. Frequent voyages were made to fetch wood from America (which ·of course was discovered by Scandinavian settlers) and tamarack timber from America has been found at Herjulfsnes. Pastureland was a matter of life or death, though the cattle must naturally be brought indoors during the winter. The sea was rich in fish and seals, the land in birds, hares, bears and reindeer—also in wolves, but these, here as elsewhere, were less popular. Thus, though hard, life was endurable.

It must be admitted, however, that the medieval chronicles are remarkably silent about distant Greenland. In about 1540, human beings were sighted there again—but for the last time. Some sort of disaster must have occurred, as we have now learnt from excavations in the old settlements and the ice-covered ground.

Eskimos were often to be found in Greenland; their presence is reported by the latest historians of the saga period. But soon after 1300 came the great Eskimo migration across Smith Sound and southwards along the west coast of Greenland. The Europeans were compelled to give up the walrus-fishing grounds which were so vital to their trade with Europe and Vestibygd had to be evacuated. They were harassed on all sides by the Eskimos in their nimble kayaks, and were finally overrun altogether.

After that, there was no Scandinavian colony in Greenland for several hundred years, until the eighteenth century, when the island was won back by Hans Egede. For a long time it remained an Eskimo settlement governed by a few Danish officials. Until the beginning of the present century, the authorities in Copenhagen deliberately opposed all attempts to hasten the spread of civilization to this primitive people. After that there was no stopping it and by this time the population had become so mixed that a cross-bred race of Eskimos and Norsemen may be said to have resulted. The fishing industry developed and other industries were modernized. Kayaks are things of the past; people prefer sound diesel-powered ships and take up-to-date measures against cold and darkness. Thule has become a well-known airfield on the Polar route.

There is one more foreign race—and this time in the heart of the Scandinavian peninsula: the Lapps, a people in no way related to the Eskimos. Their ancestors are believed to have been reindeer hunters who arrived from the south-east in prehistoric times. Gradually every Lapp family came to regard certain herds of reindeer as its own, and marked the beasts' ears accordingly. Little by little they changed from hunters to herdsmen of the reindeer, migrating in the spring with their animals to a distance of 200 miles or more inland. There, in the mountains, the summer climate was the most suitable for the herds; and in the autumn men and animals moved down again to the sheltered plains and forests. The way was always the same, village by village, family beside family, in a long, advancing front.

The Vikings, in their enterprising pursuit of trade, brought prosperity and metals to the Lapps for a brief period, after which they fell back into almost complete isolation. During the eighteenth century they were converted to Christianity by energetic Swedish missionaries, but in other respects they remained faithful to their own particular culture.

Now, in the middle of the twentieth century, the great change has come even to the Lapps. They sell their beasts to the slaughterhouses and are paid in cash, with which they buy the usual comforts of civilization. In 1912, for the first time, the women of one *Sita* spent the summer in their permanent winter quarters instead of setting off to the mountains with their menfolk. Soon the seasonal migration of entire families was a thing of the past. The men now follow their herds on skis and by modern means of transport and are adapting themselves more and more to modern techniques. The romance of Lapland will soon vanish from the list of tourist attractions. The people still wear their national costume in everyday life, but their whole interest is directed towards a complete transformation of their customs: permanent schools for the children, local self-government, building loans, problems raised by the construction of power-stations and dams, stock-breeding, and the need to come to terms with social developments in present-day Sweden.

Such is Scandinavia—a diversity of nations, cultural traditions and ways of life, a microcosm of Europe, differences on all sides. Yet it forms a single entity, and the time has come to speak of that.

We are always brought back, in describing Scandinavia, to the original community formed by its inhabitants—to the Viking Age, which had *one* language, *one* religion, *one* social structure and made *one* united contribution to world history. The dragon ships with their transverse sails laid the foundation for the great European expansion.

Colonies were founded on many points of the Baltic coastline—at Libau, Apuole, Elbing, and in Finland for example. The Norwegians thrust westward in the same way. In 793 their attack on Lindisfarne Abbey off the east coast of England brought these pirates, as they were at first, to the attention of the earliest Western chroniclers who reported them for posterity.

Originally the Norsemen confined themselves to sporadic raids, the crew of a ship attacking some monastery on the coast. But before long they began striving for a foothold in distant lands. The Vikings established colonies in all directions. Ireland came under Norwegian domination as early as the 820s. Friesland was a Continental bridgehead. A few ships made their way down the Russian rivers to the Black Sea and Byzantium. Later they gained control of these rivers, and founded their first State on the Dnieper, with Kiev as its capital. In 911, Normandy became a fief of the Normans. The *Danelag*, or 'Five Boroughs', was established as a strong Viking domain in the east of England. Iceland, Greenland and North America were discovered and the first two of them, as we have seen, were actually colonized. Normandy became the springboard for further progress by the Vikings; in 1066, William the Conqueror invaded England; other enterprising Normans went as far as Sicily where they encountered some of their compatriots who had come by the eastern route to take service with the Byzantine Emperor and were now fighting for him. This was colonization at a great distance from home. We usually think of the Vikings either as heroes or as bloodthirsty desperadoes. But neither view conveys the measure of their economic and psychological influence on international history.

31

During the eleventh century the powers of these seamen began to decline. United Scandinavia split into three States. Indeed, we could no longer call it Scandinavia except that the desire for unity survived. It is important to remember this for a proper understanding of Northern Europe.

A law of one of the Swedish provinces in the early Middle Ages prescribed that 'He who kills a Dane or a Norwegian shall pay a fine of nine marks. . . . He who kills a Southman (i.e. German) or an Englishman shall pay a fine of four marks'. So the life of a Scandinavian citizen was considered to be worth more than twice that of any other foreigner. In the thirteenth century, love of Scandinavia's pagan past was kept alive by Snorri the Icelander and Saxo the Dane and presumably it still existed in Sweden, though no chronicler came forward there.

The idea of a union between the northern States was a familiar and accepted notion. Sweden and Norway came together as early as 1319 under King Magnus Eriksson and remained united in one way or another over a long period.

Then came a fully fledged Scandinavian Union. Margrete, daughter of Valdemar Atterdag, having inherited the thrones of Denmark and Norway, was begged to extend her rule to Sweden as well. In 1389 the 'Union of Kalmar' was drafted, providing for a Scandinavian Federation with local laws, but joint leadership and foreign policy. No final document has come down to us, only a written draft. Margrete ruled wisely and energetically until 1412 over an empire which extended from Karelia in the east to Greenland in the west—the most extensive of any in Europe.

In the fourteenth century the idea of union remained so vivid that Sweden often merely elected a Regent. Archbishop Jöns Bengtsson Oxenstierna laid his insignia in front of the high altar in the cathedral at Uppsala, vowing never to wear them again until the Union was concluded, though in the meantime he showed no great reluctance to rule alone from the palace at Stockholm. There were others who hoped for a purely Swedish King—in some cases, themselves. The peasants repeatedly took a hand—armed or unarmed—in these developments.

At last, in 1471, there was a decisive battle—at Brunkeberg, the spot where Stockholm's five skyscrapers now stand. The Danes were fighting against the Swedes, with Swedish leaders on both sides. The Danes were defeated, and for a long time there was no more talk of union.

This battle is recorded by Bernt Notke, the woodcarver from Lübeck, in his finest work, *St George and the Dragon*, which is in the main church in Stockholm. St George stands for Sweden, the Princess, shown praying for her hero, signifies the city of Stockholm, and the wicked dragon . . . shall be left nameless!

Fifty years later, King Christian II of Denmark captured Stockholm. He is still known in Sweden as Christian the Tyrant, for he shed rivers of blood in the market-place in front of the castle. It was the peasants, led by Gustav Vasa, who drove him away.

After this there was perpetual war between the brother nations which came to a head during their period of international power in the seventeenth century. King Karl Gustav X with his battle-hardened soldiers was in Poland in 1658. Suddenly he swept across North Germany and through Schleswig-Holstein into Denmark, where, from the island of Funen, he could look across the Great Belt to Zealand. Whereupon, on 6 February there set in such an exceptionally cold spell that the King with his whole army was able to march to Copenhagen

VIII   OSLO, THE TOWN HALL

on foot! His three thousand horsemen were followed next day by the infantry and artillery. The peace terms were dictated before the end of the month. Not until 1814 did the continual warfare between Sweden and Denmark come to an end.

The old hatred of the hereditary enemy is recorded in many figures of speech even today. The Danes declare that the man beneath the equestrian statue of Christian V is a Swede. This is a gratifying retort to Bernt Notke's dragon. In schoolboy slang the verb *schweden* means to shirk or cheat. An old saw declares 'He is poor, honest and Swedish and what little he has he got by stealing'. On the other hand, the Swedish dictionary defines 'danish' as 'false, faithless'; and the cry of 'Danish noddle' has led to many bloody noses.

Nowadays when we aggravate or tease one another across the frontier, we do it in a friendly, neighbourly spirit. For instance, a Swede may describe a man from across his western boundary as *'en norsk norrman fran Norge'*, making fun of the Norwegian tendency to exaggerated patriotism, while the latter will ape the unfamiliar accent of those who come from the country of *'Swääärje'*.

There were many harbingers of the modern understanding among the Scandinavian States. In a speech he made in London in 1792, J. S. Sneedorff stressed the need for closer union between the three northern countries. Scandinavian Literary Associations were founded. The ancient northern poetry and mythology were sought out. In 1810, Grundtvig wrote a play entitled *Is a Northern Union Desirable?* In 1829, Esaias Tegnér, the Swedish poet, crowned the Danish writer, Adam Oehlenschläger, with a laurel wreath at Lund, saying 'The day of division is over—it should never have existed in the free, boundless world of the mind . . . so take your crown from a brother's hand'.

In February 1838 the Öresjön froze over, but with a result different from that of 180 years before. Some Danish students proceeded to walk over the ice on a fraternal visit to Lund; halfway across they met a group of Swedish students who had set out with the same idea. Romantic students' speeches were made at Copenhagen and two days later at Lund. The two groups met again during the summer and in 1843 these sentimental ecstasies culminated in a big sea-trip to Uppsala. On the way, the students naturally paid a visit to the castle at Kalmar, only to find that it was going to rack and ruin and that Queen Margrete's throne had been sold for a paltry sum. Emotion reached its height at the Kings' Mounds at Old Uppsala.

Meanwhile, these future civil servants and scientists had been struck by a brilliant idea. In 1845, one hundred and forty-four Norwegians came to the students' meeting at Copenhagen, despite the fact that they were striving for independence. In 1856 the last of these students' meetings was held at Old Uppsala. The participants called for complete inner freedom and independence, but with cries of 'Long live the political unity of the North!'

King Oscar I received the students at Drottningholm Castle with the historic words:

'In future, war between the Scandinavian brothers will be impossible.'

This prophecy has been fulfilled, although the Prussian war against Denmark in 1864 brought bitter disillusionment. Volunteers did come to fight for Denmark, but the general mood was remarkably listless and Sweden remained neutral while the south-western corner of Scandinavia was lost.

So ended the union of the northern peoples. Or rather, so ended their idealistic transports. What was now needed was a more matter-of-fact spirit, the hardships of the twentieth century, and a determination to achieve real mutual understanding. Men should seek to realize ideals not through power politics, but by adapting themselves to the needs of time and place.

As we have already seen, the standard of living of the Danish peasants and farmers rose steadily. They gained their freedom. They developed their bright, optimistic outlook. They bred their world-famous cattle and fattened pigs, finding these more profitable than corn-growing. They formed co-operatives for working purposes. They were eager reformers, on excellent terms with the radical townsmen. And so it was that a *Venstre*, or democratic Left party came to power as early as 1870. Norway's united population, too, declared for democracy at an early stage. Finland followed as an independent country and Iceland joined the movement.

Strangely enough, the Swedes took longer because, perhaps, of their firm belief in established authority. It is characteristic of Sweden to bring everything into the vast framework of the State—even the social services, regulation of labour, old age pensions and health insurance—just as the nonconformist sects co-operate with the established Church and atheists are expected to hold morning prayers in schools. The national home (*Folkhemmet*) is being steadily built up. The five Scandinavian peoples have been drawn closer together by the similarity of their democratic institutions.

In all five countries, peasants and workers hold a remarkably high proportion of parliamentary seats. This fact usually passes unnoticed, but it is of the greatest importance, for in other countries the majority of parliamentarians come from the 'middle' and professional classes. In France, the legal lights are masterly orators. They love controversy. They cut brilliant figures in Parliament with their arguments, they launch surprise attacks, they bewilder people, they appeal to the passions, they goad the other members, they transform the theme of the debate into a question of life or death.

The Scandinavians are brought up more soberly; their peasants and workers have little experience of rhetoric and are not given to impassioned speech. Their discussions are sober, rather laboured and lacking in brilliance, though at Copenhagen the 'living Word' may sometimes give them a little colour and liveliness. But even a small display of temperament would disturb the confident, unruffled proceedings. Unintentional humour is the kind which is preferred. Scandinavian parliamentary activity draws its strength from quite different factors—it is based on meticulous attention to the problems concerned and on the spirit of friendly co-operation that prevails everywhere.

Senior civil servants are eligible for Parliament, a thing that is forbidden in many countries. As a result, the Scandinavian assemblies have the advantage of great familiarity with administrative matters. A senior civil servant is entitled to criticize his government, in other words his superiors, quite freely in Parliament. This would be out of the question if there were any direct appeal to the emotions; it only becomes possible when they are repressed, or at least subordinated to the public interest.

The television camera is sometimes a disturbing intruder in parliamentary life. On one occasion two members of opposing parties were having a friendly chat, when they suddenly realized that the camera was trained on them. They hastily began to scowl at each other, but the public had understood the situation—and laughed. Party opponents call one another by their Christian names, lunch together, and have no hostile feelings at the ordinary human level. Inflammatory theories are kept in the background, members try to be entirely practical, always ready to come to terms with a view to adjusting social inequalities.

These are basic elements in the Scandinavian attitude towards life and milestones marking the progress of Scandinavian co-operation—now that students' romanticism and the desire for power politics have been left behind. In 1914 the three Nordic Kings met at Malmö to agree upon a joint policy of neutrality, and in 1939 occurred a similar meeting, at which Finland also was represented. Since 1945 their Home Secretaries and Foreign Ministers have met regularly and given one another guidance in all important matters. Denmark, Norway and Iceland are members of NATO, while Finland's line is determined by its treaty with Russia. Sweden has been able to maintain its strict neutrality between East and West, combined with a genuine sense of responsibility. That is the true Scandinavian spirit, in which the whole nation joins.

Renunciation is often a condition of successful co-existence among individuals and nations. Sweden gave up the union with Norway, and later surrendered the Åland Islands to Finland. After the question had been aired at The Hague, Norway surrendered Greenland. Denmark and Finland have withdrawn their claim to various border territories. The Scandinavian countries are politically mature enough to follow this last difficult path.

We hope and believe that Europe has now left all forms of nationalism behind it. But it is essential for the different peoples to show tolerance to one another, for each of them has its particular wishes, its own sensitive points, interests and grounds for resentment.

We should not try even to cure foreign nations of their irritating characteristics or bad habits, for it takes a whole combination of qualities to build up a national character. A nation survives and creates by making use of its entire personality. It is as wrong to mutilate that as to dominate individuals. Besides, differences in national character are a constant source of mutual enrichment, both among Scandinavians and among Europeans in general.

Variety is an outstanding characteristic of Scandinavia, as of Europe. We must hope that, within a co-ordinated system, it will remain so. An international union may have a fixed structure and even a number of supra-national organizations. On the other hand it may be so elastic as to have no element of compulsion about it and still succeed, as in Scandinavia. That is a matter of circumstances. The Scandinavian example shows that the essential condition of survival for a community of peoples is a deeply rooted sense of human fellowship.

ARCTIC OCEAN

North Cape

Tromsö

FINNMARK

Lofoten *Narvik* *Kilpisjärvi* *Inari* *L. Inari*

Kiruna

LAPLAND

Bodö

Saltfjord LAPLAND

Svartisen

NORWEGIAN SEA

Korgen

Oulu

NORRLAND

FINLAND

ÅNGERMANLAND

Koli

Moldefjord *Trondheim*

Aursundet *Vasa*

Trolltindene

Geirangerfjord *Savonlinna*

Sognefjord SWEDEN *Säynätsalo*

JOTUNHEIMEN *Tampere*

Borgund Gulf of Bothnia

Vøringsfoss *Vuoksenniska*

Bergen NORWAY *Siljan*

Haukeliseter *Turku* *L. Ladoga*

Rauland *Helsinki*

TELEMARK *Oslo* SVEALAND *Uppsala* Gulf of Finland

Stavanger *Rottneros* *Täby* *Åland*

Heddal *L. Väner* *Strängnäs* *Stockholm*

Kragerø

Göta Canal

L. Vätter *Vadstena*

Skagen

Göteborg *Visby*

GÖTALAND *Gotland*

DENMARK *Ålborg*

Randers *Kalmar* *Öland*

Århus *Hälsingborg*

NORTH SEA

Fanø *Helsingør* SKÅNE

Vejle *Lund*

Ribe *Malmö*

Odense *Copenhagen (København)*

Bornholm BALTIC SEA

150   Miles

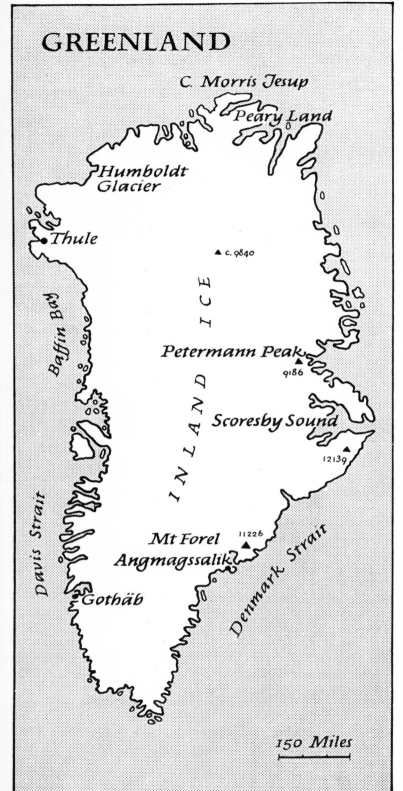

GREENLAND

C. Morris Jesup

Peary Land

Humboldt Glacier

Thule

Baffin Bay

▲ c. 9840

INLAND ICE

Davis Strait

Petermann Peak
9186

Scoresby Sound

12139

Mt Forel
Angmagssalik
11226

Denmark Strait

Gothåb

150 Miles

ICELAND

Siglufjördur

Húsavík

Oxnadalur

Faxaflói

Reykjavik

Vatna Jökull
6952

Hekla

Vestmannaeyjar

SPITSBERGEN

North East Land

5636

Olga Strait

West Spitsbergen

Stor Fjord

Edge Island

150 Miles

NOTES

Colour Plates

I NORWAY. Ålesund (pop. *c.* 20,000), half-way between Bergen and Trondheim on the west coast of Norway, stands on the islands of Nørvøy, Aspøy and Heissa, far out in the coastal belt of rocky islands. The town formerly consisted chiefly of wooden buildings, but was rebuilt in stone after a disastrous fire in 1904. Ålesund is Norway's principal fishing port, the home of a large cod and herring fleet, with an important fish-processing industry which is one of the oldest and most productive sectors of the Norwegian economy. Fish products represent approximately one-fifth of Norway's exports.

II ICELAND. A mud volcano and hot springs, with fountains of steam shooting up in the background (cf. pls. 4, 5). In the Faeroes, which are geologically closely related to Iceland, volcanic activity soon became extinct, but it continues in Iceland to this day. Since the island was first settled, thirty active volcanoes have been located, and an eruption occurs on an average every five years. About one-third of all the lava thrown up on the earth since the year 1500 is to be found in Iceland. The island's most famous volcano, Hekla, last erupted in 1947.

III ICELAND. Waterfall over a vertical rock-face of basalt columns. Iceland consists largely of young volcanic rock and about half the island is covered with a layer of basalt.

IV DENMARK. On the Nyhavn in Copenhagen, a narrow channel between the harbour and the Kongens Nytorv. From the bright façades of the houses, many in the old gabled style, one would hardly suspect by day that this is the ill-famed 'harbour quarter', with the whirl of nocturnal amusements common to every great port.

V DENMARK. Harvesting the corn. Windmills are still to be found in many parts of the country (cf. pl. 61).

VI SWEDEN. The Lule Älv, in Swedish Lapland, is one of the many rivers on which vast numbers of logs from the forests in the interior of northern Sweden are floated down to the Gulf of Bothnia, where they are shipped abroad or milled (cf. pls. 124–6).

VII SWEDEN. In front of Stockholm's concert hall stands the Orpheus Fountain, one of the finest works of the Swedish sculptor, Carl Milles (1936) (cf. pl. 100). The skyscrapers in the background are part of Stockholm's new central business quarter.

VIII NORWAY. The new Town Hall on Oslo harbour, built between 1931 and 1950 (cf. pls. 138, 139).

Monochrome Plates
ICELAND
Plates 1–17

After Great Britain, Iceland is Europe's largest island (39,716 sq. miles; greatest distance north and south, 180 miles; greatest distance east and west, about 300 miles). It lies between latitude 63° north and the Arctic circle, which it just touches in the north, and between longitude 13° and 24° west. Geologically Iceland is part of a basalt formation stretching from Scotland beyond the Faeroes towards Greenland. Iceland is also noted for the greatest volcanic activity and the largest glaciers in Europe (Vatna Jökull, 3,475 sq. miles; in all, glaciers cover an area of more than 5,000 sq. miles). The interior of the island consists largely of a barren, volcanic plateau, covered with ice, lava and ash and is accessible only with great difficulty. Only some 386 sq. miles. of this area are arable. Settlements (pop. *c.* 170,000) are confined to the coastal areas and the most densely populated parts are the south-west and the south, where the influence of the Gulf Stream, to which Iceland owes its amazingly mild climate, is strongest.

Iceland's discovery by St Brendan in the sixth century still belongs to the realm of legend. The first settlement by Irish monks dates from the eighth century. In 874 colonists arrived from Norway—nobles who, by emigrating, sought to escape the domination of King Harald Fairhair. The colony's rapid progress led to the founding of an independent republic in the year 930 and at the turn of the century Iceland was converted to Christianity. In 1280 came union with Norway, as a result of which, in 1380, Iceland came, together with that country, under the Danish crown, where it remained until 1943. Since that date Iceland has been a republic, with the oldest parliament in the world, the *Althing*, which was founded in 930 and has two Houses. The language has changed so little in relation to that of the *Edda* and the old sagas that even today they are read in the original.

1 The HAÍFOSS—Iceland's numerous waterfalls are a typical feature of its geologically young and little-eroded landscape.

2 HUSAVÍK (pop. *c.* 2,000), a small trading and fishing port in northern Iceland.

3 REYKJAVÍK, the 'smoky bay', so called by the first settlers on account of the steam from the many hot springs in the south-west part of the island, where Iceland's capital stands today. Reykjavík is the heart of the country, the link with the outside world, the seat of the University, the business centre. It owes its rapid growth to its favourable situation. Lying at the head of the only really ice-free bay between the two main catchment areas in the north-west and the south-east, it was the ideal centre both for agriculture and for the fishing fleet. By European standards Reykjavík is only a small town (about 70,000 inhabitants) but by having to fulfil the functions of a capital city it has grown far more important than its population would indicate. Of all capitals in the world, Reykjavík, in relation to the population of the country as a whole, has the greatest concentration of inhabitants—about 41 per cent. As late as 1850 the population was only 1,200 (in 1801 it had been 301) and even since 1940 it has almost doubled. This rapid development reflects the growth of industries about half of whose products, measured by value, are manufactured in the capital.

4–5 HVERAGERDI is a small place in the south on the lower slopes of the Hengill range. The local hot springs are used for growing hothouse fruit, vegetables and flowers. The water pipes can be seen in the foreground. The GRÝTA (pl. 5) is a hot spring in the neighbourhood which spouts up to a height of 33 ft. every two hours. It has been estimated that Iceland's approximately 700 geysers together throw up 330 gallons of hot water per second. Iceland possesses a gigantic potential source of energy in the numerous thermal zones situated chiefly in the geologically young volcanic areas. Chemically speaking, the springs are of two kinds—acid and alkaline—differing greatly in appearance and in smell. The acid springs are sulphurous. They are often mud springs with the most amazing range of colours, from bright red and brown to dull white and yellow. The alkaline springs are more widespread. They are probably formed by seepage which, after coming into contact with hot rock, returns to the surface again. These natural sources of energy have long been used in Iceland for household purposes (at Reykholt a thirteenth-century bathtub is still to be seen). Recently a start has been made on exploiting this energy by modern technical means. The largest undertaking is the Reykjavík hot-water supply, which today serves more than half the inhabitants. As at Hveragerdi, almost all the hothouses in the country use this 'free' source of energy.

6 In the Öxnadalur (northern Iceland). Since olden days the road from Reykjavík to Akreyri, the 'northern capital', has run through this valley.

7 The early settlers in Iceland were farmers and Iceland long remained a land of farmers. Even fishing was until not so long ago only a sideline to be engaged in during the months when there was little to do on the farms, especially in the south with its abundant winter catch.

Compared with the other Scandinavian countries, agriculture in Iceland has two unique features: there are no wooded areas, and cereal crops cannot be grown (recent trials with oats have produced good results but they are still only at the experimental stage). Farming in Iceland has always been based chiefly on sheep and cattle raising on natural, uncultivated pastures (cf. pls. 9 and 10). Thus, Icelandic farmers have always been to some extent nomadic and it may well be that their love of folktales, poetry and the old sagas is bound up with this feature of their lives. Agriculture in Iceland is now equipped with every modern device. OLD FARMHOUSES, like that depicted here, have become rare. This one is built according to the ancient custom of keeping in the heat with turf. Sods of dried turf are piled up and matted firmly together to make thick walls. Each room forms a 'house' of its own, gable to gable with its neighbours.

8 The VESTMANNAEYJAR or 'Westman' Islands are off the south coast of Iceland. Several platform-like islands falling sharply to the sea surround the larger island of Heimaey on which the chief town, Kaupstadur, is situated.

This is important as a base for the small diesel-driven Icelandic fishing boats, while the port of Reykjavík serves the larger steamers. These islands, being even more under the influence of the Gulf Stream than the south-west coast, have the highest average temperature in Iceland, namely 5.5°C (42°F).

9-10 The raising of livestock, especially sheep rearing, has always been the backbone of Icelandic farming. In 1957 sheep numbered 766,000, cattle 49,300 and horses 33,300. While cattle raising occurs mainly in the south, sheep are reared chiefly in the north and north-east, where vast uninhabited grasslands are to be found. From June onwards, the sheep are left without shepherds in the highlands, far from the farms. About 10 September the *göngumenn* or 'sheep-seekers', set off under an experienced leader to bring the flocks back from the high pastures, often more than 60 miles away. Several days, perhaps a whole week, later, they drive the great flock of several thousand sheep into the herding pens (pl. 9). Each owner knows his own sheep from the distinctive cut made in the ear. When the process of handing the sheep over to their owners (in Icelandic: *dregid i dilka*) is over, a great celebration begins, with singing and dancing and much drinking of Icelandic brandy.

11 SIGLUFJÖRDUR (pop. c. 3,000), on the north coast just below the Arctic circle, is Iceland's main herring port. Icelandic waters are among the most plentifully stocked with fish in the world. Representing 97 per cent of Iceland's exports, fishing and fish processing are a vital feature of the country's foreign trade. The Government has always vigorously upheld Icelandic fishing interests (in 1958, in spite of strong opposition, above all from England, they extended the fishing limits for foreign craft to 12 miles from the coast). The development of Icelandic fisheries into an important part of the economy is of recent date; it began only with the technical progress that marked the end of the nineteenth century. Before then fishing had been for centuries of purely local importance. The main catches are cod in the southern waters and herring in the north. Haddock, catfish, halibut and whale are also caught. In addition to fishing the home waters, the Icelandic fishing fleet exploits distant fishing grounds, off the coast of Greenland for instance, or around Bear Island. Fish processing in Iceland has undergone a significant change in the last century. Whereas salted fish and fresh fish on ice were once the most important exports, thanks to modern technical advances deep-frozen fish is now by far the largest item in the processing industry

and the export trade, although, as this picture shows, salt herring is not yet quite out of the running.

12 These singular lumps of basalt, weathered to a smooth, round shape, are found near SELFOSS, a little settlement in the south.

13 The SKOGAFOSS, in southern Iceland, which drops more than 200 ft. over a sheer wall of basalt, is one of the country's largest and finest waterfalls.

14 *Selveidimenn* is the Icelandic name for the SEAL-HUNTERS, seen here returning with their catch. Seal-hunting on a small scale is carried on at several points of the coast, some 300 adult seals and 3,000 young animals being killed each year.

15 River valley in the Landmannalaugar region (southern Iceland), lying to the east of Iceland's best-known volcano, Hekla.

16-17 Among Iceland's rather scanty fauna, sea-birds are the most numerous; there are some 200 species, seventy of which nest on the island in enormous numbers. They are still caught today on the bird rocks that ring Iceland and on the bird colonies of Drangey and Grimsey Islands in the north (cf. pl. 8). In many places men let themselves down the rock face by ropes, amid the indescribable screeching of the birds, to take the guillemots' eggs from the nests. It is not unusual at the right season for a man indulging in this dangerous but fascinating task to take several hundred birds and as many eggs in a day.

16. The gannet is a sea-bird which remains on land only during the breeding season, as here on the island of SÚLNASKER.

17. The BLACK-BACKED GULL (Larus marinus) is also at home in Iceland. It owes its name to the dark feathers on its wings and back.

Iceland's isolation is such that the first settlers found only one mammal there—the polar fox. The position (apart from domestic animals) has scarcely changed since. Rats and mice came ashore from ships and in the latter half of the eighteenth century a herd of reindeer was brought from Norway; their descendants have returned to their wild state and still live in the highlands north of the Vatna Jökull. Some mink escaped from captivity in the 1930s and, now wild, they are multiplying rapidly and becoming a serious threat to the bird population.

DENMARK

Plates 18–69

The Kingdom of Denmark embraces, in addition to Denmark proper, the Faeroe Islands and Greenland which are governed as Danish provinces. Denmark proper, with its 16,602 sq. miles, is by far the smallest of the Scandinavian countries. It consists of the Jutland peninsula, which makes up two-thirds of the total area, and some 500 islands of which only about 100 are inhabited. The largest of these are Zealand, Funen, Lolland-Falster and Bornholm. With a population of approximately four and a half million and an average density of 267 per sq. mile, Denmark is many times more thickly populated than the other Scandinavian countries. Denmark is the meeting point of Central and Northern Europe: its natural conditions are broadly speaking Central European, its language is Scandinavian, while its culture and economy show affinities with both sides.

The geological formation of Denmark goes almost directly back to the Ice Age whose deposits and formations produced the present flat or gently un-dulating landscape. A terminal moraine which runs through the whole length of Jutland, marking the furthest point to which the ice once advanced, still forms a clearly recognizable boundary between certain villages and agricultural districts. The subsoil is of chalk and lime, which come to the surface along some stretches of the coast. The coastline of the islands and of eastern Jutland (total length 4,500 miles) is deeply indented in contrast to the marshes and dunes of the west Jutland coast.

The Danes are a Germanic people who came from Sweden to Jutland by way of the islands in the Iron Age. In the course of history Denmark was several times the ruling power in Scandinavia, most markedly during the period of the Kalmar Union, when both Norway and Sweden had a personal link with the Danish Crown. Before then, as a result of the wide-spread expeditions of the Vikings since the early ninth century, the Kingdom of Canute the Great had embraced the whole of England and Norway in the eleventh century and the Valdemar kings had ruled extensive territories in north Germany and the Baltic. Rivalry with Sweden following that country's with-drawal from the Kalmar Union (1523) and later the opposition of England led to Denmark's gradual decline from its position as a great Power—a decline determined finally by the loss of Norway in 1814.

Denmark has been a constitutional monarchy since 1849 (after 200 years of absolute rule); legislative power is in the hands of the Danish Parliament—the *Folketing* —whose 179 members are elected every four years.

18–19 The FAEROE ISLANDS, or Föroyar, as they are called in Faeroese, are situated in the North Atlantic between latitude 61°24' and 62°24' north and longitude 6°15' and 7°41' west. The eighteen inhabited and twelve uninhabited islands of the group cover a total area of 540 sq. miles and had a population in 1958 of about 32,000.

The islands form part of a vast basalt deposit produced by volcanic eruption in the Tertiary era, extending from Scotland beyond Iceland to Greenland and break-ing the surface of the sea in a few places only. Layers of basalt lava alternating with strata of tuff, together with the troughs and steep mountain formations left by the Ice Age are features of the landscape. Characteristic of the islands are the numerous parallel fjords running from north-west to south-east, the most striking of which divides the two largest islands, Streymoy (144 sq. miles) and Eysturoy (110 sq. miles). On Streymoy is the capital Thorshavn (pop. *c.* 6,000). The nearest inhabited land to the Faeroes are the Shetland Islands, 180 miles away. The distance from Copenhagen is 780 miles.

The islands, to which Irish monks brought Christi-anity as early as the sixth century, were colonized by Norwegian seafarers in the ninth century. In 1380 the Faeroes came to Denmark as a result of the Norwegian–Danish Union and remained attached to Denmark even after the Union was dissolved in 1814. Since 1948 they have been to a large extent independent. The Faeroe dialect spoken there is a cross between Norwegian and Icelandic. The climate, which allows of practically no agriculture, has always led the inhabitants to rely on two main sources of livelihood, fishing and sheep-rearing. The name of the islands, which means 'sheep islands' is an indication of this. The sheep number roughly 60,000.

18. The DRANGUR ROCK, a natural rock arch in the west of the island of Vágar. The slanting upper surface is overgrown with grass on which in summer sheep graze, being hauled up and down by means of ropes. In the background is the island of Tindholm (Tooth Island). The coastal cliffs reach enormous heights; the rock face at Enniberg in the north of the island of Vidoy, for example, rises to more than 2,200 ft. and is thus one of the highest (if not the highest) cliffs in the world. The narrow ledges of these cliffs, like

certain spots in Iceland (cf. pl. 16), serve as nesting-places for millions of sea-birds, especially guillemots.

19. This farm at SAKSEN, on the Pollur Fjord (Island of Stremoy), gives an impression of the primitive simplicity and isolation of a settlement in the Faeroes, untouched by civilization to an extent that is rarely found today. Farms in the islands, as elsewhere in Scandinavia, consist of several independent buildings. The living quarters, with the chimney, are seen on the left.

20 Off the port of Esbjerg on the west coast of Jutland is the 10-mile-long island of FANØ. Its great stretch of beach makes it a place of international bathing resorts, of which the largest is Vesterhausbad (cf. pl. 67). The island's chief town is the fishing port of Nordby on the east coast. The dimensions and ground-plan of the single-frame houses in the fishing village of Sønderho on Fanø have become the model for a widespread type of modern family dwelling in the traditional Danish style.

21–38 COPENHAGEN, on the Sound, on the east side of the island of Zealand, though now by far the largest trading and industrial city in Denmark, did not become the recognized centre of Danish life until relatively late, despite its commanding position. It was not until 1445 that the kings transferred their residence from Roskilde to Copenhagen. Archbishop Absalon of Roskilde, was the founder of Copenhagen, which is mentioned for the first time in 1043, as 'Havn'. The town's importance as a trading centre, owing to its favourable position on the route from the North Sea to the Baltic, is reflected in its name. In the Middle Ages it was already known as 'Købmannehavn', or 'Merchants' town'. Today some 40 per cent of Danish industry is centred in Copenhagen which, with 1,250,000 inhabitants, contains about a quarter of the population of Denmark. More than two-thirds of the total turnover of the Danish ports passes this way, chiefly through the Free Port, which dates from 1894. Copenhagen's cultural amenities and art collections make it at the same time the cultural and intellectual centre of Danish life.

21. The great centrally situated MARMORKIRKE or 'Marble Church', with its lofty, frescoed dome, was begun by Frederick V in 1749 to mark the 300th anniversary of the rule of the House of Oldenburg. The original design was by the architect N. Eigtved (1701–54), but the work was broken off for a long time and only completed in 1878–94, by Fr. Meldahl (1827–1908)—an earlier attempt by the French architect

N. Jardin having failed for lack of funds. Both as regards its site and its architecture, the church is closely related to the Amalienborg (pls. 22, 23).

22, 23. The AMALIENBORG, seat of the royal family since the palace of Christiansborg was destroyed by fire in 1754, is one of the finest monuments that the eighteenth century has left to Europe. Frederick V, who also began the near-by Marmorkirke (pl. 21), handed certain estates over to four nobles, on condition that they had the Amalienborg built entirely according to the plans of N. Eigtved, a pupil of Pöppelmann. The four main edifices composing the design are placed diagonally and linked to form an octagon. The palace was built between 1749 and 1760. Drawing inspiration from Italian and even more from French styles, Eigtved evolved a restrained, elegant Danish rococo which achieved its finest expression in the Amalienborg; this is the greatest example of Danish eighteenth-century architecture. When the king is in residence, the ceremony of the Changing of the Guard, with its military band and historic uniforms, takes place every day at noon in the palace yard. Of the four main blocks composing the Amalienborg, the one in the north-east corner of the courtyard is the residence of the present King.

24. KNIPPELSBRO, a lever draw-bridge with a span of 95 ft., links the island palace of Christiansborg with the part of Copenhagen known as Christianshavn, on the island of Amager, which was laid out in 1618, during the reign of Christian IV (cf. pl. 27).

25. View across the harbour from close beside the Knippelsbro (pl. 24), looking towards the Strandgade, which runs parallel to the sea front, behind the houses, and the spire of the Frelsers Kirke, with its characteristic spiral staircase (cf. pl. 27).

26. Among the Danish rulers of the sixteenth and seventeenth centuries, Christian IV was the most active in planning and steadfast in promoting the development of Copenhagen from a medieval town into a Renaissance metropolis. A monument to his efforts is the Copenhagen EXCHANGE, which he had built between 1619 and 1625 by the brothers Lorenz and Hans van Steenwinkel the Younger. It is modelled on the Dutch Renaissance style which also influenced other buildings sponsored by Christian IV, such as the Palace of Frederiksborg (cf. pl. 45).

27. In Christianshavn on the island of Amager stands the FRELSERS KIRKE (Church of the Redeemer), built to the design of Lambert van Haven (1630–95),

43

King Christian IV's leading architect, in the years 1682–96, when the tendency was towards the Dutch Reformed Church architecture of the time. Its tower, the tallest in the city after that of the Town Hall, is original even among the many towers of Copenhagen: the spire is formed by a steeply rising outside spiral staircase (pl. 25). The most striking features of the interior decoration are the baroque organ of 1698 and the high altar by N. Tessin the Younger, the builder of the Palace of Stockholm (pl. 92).

28. The GRUNDTVIGSKIRKE on the Copenhagen Bispebjerg (Bishop's Mount) in the north-west of the city, is dedicated to the memory of Nicolai Frederik Severin Grundtvig (1783–1872), one of the most truly national figures of nineteenth-century Denmark. As a clergyman, poet, philologist, pedagogue, historian and politician he led the way, after Denmark's decline as a great Power, in laying the foundations for a new cultural policy directed above all towards instilling new life into rural society.

The Grundtvigskirke was built between 1921 and 1940. The original plans by P. V. Jensen Klint (1853–1920) provided for the tower only, which was dedicated in 1927. It was his son Kaare Klint (1888–1954) who enlarged it into a complete church. The general concept, that of an enormously enlarged Danish village church, provoked some criticism. It represents the culmination of a romantic, nationalist trend in Danish architecture.

29. The TIVOLI, in the centre of Copenhagen, laid out in 1843 by Georg Carstensen (1812–56) on the site of old fortifications, is perhaps Europe's most celebrated amusement park. The vast gardens with their concert, exhibition and dance-halls, their shops and restaurants, offer a wide variety of entertainment to young and old. The theatre specializes in impromptu comedies after the style of the Commedia dell'Arte.

30. The Copenhagen ROYAL BALLET enjoys a world-wide reputation. Originating with the seventeenth-century Court Ballet, its connection with the stage dates from as early as 1722, when the first permanent Danish theatre was opened. In 1771 the Royal Ballet School was founded, with the Frenchman Pierre Laurant as its first Director. In later years too the development of the ballet into a modern company was largely due to foreign talent and above all to Auguste Bournonville (1805–79). To him the Royal Ballet owes most of its classical repertory and the influence of his personal style can still be felt today. Of the fifty or so ballets staged by him, ten are still performed as

cherished features of the repertory. In the twentieth century it was at last a Dane, Harald Lander, who led the ballet on to new successes.

31. The GAMMEL STRAND at Copenhagen is the site of the morning fish-market.

32, 33. In the seventeenth century, Christian IV had the little low houses of NYBODER built as homes for seamen and their families—an early example of a 'housing estate', reminiscent of similar schemes launched by the Hanseatic towns and by the Fuggers of Augsburg.

34. One of the favourite walks in Copenhagen is along the Promenade, or Langelinie, which follows the harbour. Here the 'Little Mermaid' (*Lille Havfrue*), a bronze by Edvard Eriksen, inspired by Hans Andersen's fairy-tale, sits not far from the elegant Langelinie Pavilion (in the background on the right), built in 1958 by the architects Eva and Nils Koppel for the Royal Danish Yacht Club.

35. The HANS CHRISTIAN ANDERSEN MEMORIAL by August Saabye (1823–1916), showing the great writer of fairy-tales in the act of telling a story, stands in the Kongens Have, the former park of the Palace of Rosenborg, built between 1608 and 1617 as a summer residence by Christian IV (cf. pl. 53).

36. Near the Pillar of Freedom (seen on the left), which was erected in 1797 in the centre of Copenhagen as a memorial to peasant emancipation, stands the 22-storey S.A.S. BUILDING. It consists of a low block housing the airline's offices and a skyscraper containing Scandinavia's largest hotel and a garage. Copenhagen, with its airport of Kastrup on the island of Amager, is a point of junction of world airlines which has taken on even more importance since S.A.S. became the first airways company to operate a regular line over the Pole to North America and East Asia.

37. The housing estate of BELLAHØJ on the outer edge of Copenhagen is the combined work of a number of architects and building firms. It was completed in 1956.

It is typical of Denmark, which is both a highly industrialized country and a land of intensive farming, that the largest of Denmark's livestock shows—of which there are about a hundred—takes place every year just beside this modern residential quarter.

38. LYNGBY, near Copenhagen, is one of those outdoor museums in whose construction and arrangement the Scandinavians show special skill and have

developed a tradition of their own (cf. pls. 54, 101–4, 146, 147). Farm buildings, utensils and fittings from all over Denmark are displayed at Lyngby in such a way that the visitor can see the original relationship of the settlement to its natural environment. This photograph shows a village smithy from Ørbæck on Funen island, built around 1845.

39 SKAGEN is Denmark's most northerly town and largest fishing port. The northernmost tip of land is Skagen Point, where the Skagerrak meets the Kattegat, at latitude 57°34′ north. At Skagen, in the last quarter of the nineteenth century, a school of painters grew up who developed a specifically Danish form of impressionism in reaction to the literary and romantic trend in painting in Denmark at the time. Their most important representative was P. S. Kroyer (1851–1909). In the dunes about a mile to the south-west of the town lies the old church of Skagen which has been buried in the drifting sand since 1775.

40 At VEDERSØ on the west coast of Jutland stands one of the many medieval village churches whose features were incorporated in the plan of the Grundtviskirke at Copenhagen (pl. 28), in this case chiefly the heavy squat tower with its characteristic pilaster strips.

Kaj Munk, the Danish poet and dramatist, spent the last twenty years of his life, until his murder by the Gestapo, as Pastor at Vedersø.

41, 43 On a headland across the harbour in the north-east of the town of Helsingør (Shakespeare's 'Elsinore'), right beside the shipyards, stands the castle of KRONBORG, 'Hamlet's castle'. On the 'platform before the castle' of Helsingør, the so-called *flagbatteri* of Kronborg, Shakespeare's Hamlet met his father's ghost. Kronborg, designed by the Flemish architect Antonius van Olbergen, was built between 1577 and 1585 in the reign of Frederick II, on the site of the old fortress of Krogen, constructed by Erik of Pomerania in the early fifteenth century. With its four wings, corner towers and impressive inner courtyard, it forms the first of a long series of palaces built by the Danish kings of the Renaissance period.

42 HELSINGØR, originally an unimportant fishing village, today an old mercantile town and port (pop. 15,000) owes its rise to its position at the narrowest part of the Sound (Øresund or Öresjön)—Hälsingborg on the Swedish side is only about 3 miles away—and to the fact that Denmark used to levy a toll at this point on all ships passing through the Sound (not until 1857 did the seafaring nations induce Denmark to commute

this for a payment of about 60 million Danish crowns). The train- and car-ferry to Hälsingborg is among the most important lines of communication between Denmark and Sweden.

44 The palace of FREDENSBORG on Zealand, the autumn residence of the royal family, was built between 1720 and 1722 under Frederick IV, as a memorial to the peace concluded between Denmark and Sweden at Frederiksborg in 1720. The King's strong preference for Italian art finds clear expression in the architecture of this palace, which was built to the design of J. C. Krieger (1683–1755). The park is considered to be one of the finest in Denmark.

45 If the Copenhagen exchange (pl. 26) is an example of Christian IV's taste for elegance in architecture, the palace of FREDERIKSBORG in north Zealand shows that the King and his architects were also masters of the heavy, monumental style. Frederiksborg (built 1602–20) is one of the greatest Renaissance palaces in Northern Europe; French in its ground-plan, Flemish in its ornamentation, it stands majestically upon three small islands in the palace lake. Much of the present building is the result of restoration undertaken according to the original plans at the instigation of J. C. Jacobsen, the brewer, after a serious fire in 1859. The palace then became the National Historical Museum.

46 The great period for the building of country mansions began in Denmark towards the middle of the sixteenth century. The *Grafenfehde* (Nobles' Feud) (1534–6) had left the aristocracy victorious over the middle-class and the peasants. At the same time the discovery of the South American silver mines brought a period of great prosperity to Europe, and most of the enormous profits accruing to Denmark found their way into the hands of the nobles. The castles of this period are an expression of the power of the Danish nobility. The EGESKOV WATER PALACE on Funen Island was built about 1550.

47–8 ROSKILDE (pop. 30,000) on Zealand, at the southern end of the Roskilde Fjord, is the former capital of Denmark. Absalon, Archbishop of Roskilde, founded Copenhagen in the twelfth century. Roskilde reached the height of its prosperity in the eleventh and twelfth centuries but soon declined in importance after 1445, when the Danish kings made Copenhagen their capital. As an old historical centre, however, Roskilde, the largest town in the interior of Zealand, still has great attraction.

47. The TOWN HALL, dating from 1884, forms an architectural ensemble with the tower of the Church of St Lawrence, which was almost entirely destroyed by fire in 1527.

48. The CATHEDRAL was begun under Bishop Absalon in 1170 on the site of an earlier church. The original plan of the brick edifice shows affinities with religious buildings of the same period in northern France. The two needle spires were added later, in 1635–6, under Christian IV. The Cathedral is the burial-place of the Danish kings, most of whom lie there, some of them in the chapels added later on the north and south sides. The porch, dating from 1440, is thought to be if not the best, at least the most delightful example of Gothic in Denmark. The high altar, with its gilded altar-piece, is Netherlandish work of the late sixteenth century. The choir-stalls date from 1420.

49. KALUNDBORG (pop. c. 9,000) on the west coast of Zealand, inside the fjord of the same name, is the terminus of the important shipping route from Århus across the Great Belt. Already an important town in the Middle Ages, Kalundborg, together with the towns of Korsør, Slagelse, Sorø and Naestved, has an important place in the long-term planning that has always been carried on in Denmark with great foresight, as a future centre of the Great Belt. The Church of Our Lady (Vor Frue Kirke), reflects the violent internal struggles of the days of the Valdemar kings. This church with its five towers was built about 1170 as a fortified church on the plan of a Greek cross. Above each arm of the cross is a tower; the larger tower in the centre collapsed in 1827 and was rebuilt in 1866.

50. The twelfth-century church of BJERNEDE near Sorø in west Zealand is the only remaining medieval round church on Denmark's largest island, whereas on Bornholm (pl. 69) four churches of this type have been preserved. Their fortress-like structure made them at the time of their building practically impregnable. Here the population sought refuge when the Wends landed from their ships to plunder the coast.

51. The SVANNINGE hills to the north of the town of Fåborg on Funen, a moraine formation popularly known as the 'Funen Alps', form the only noteworthy rising ground on the second-largest Danish island (1,149 sq. miles). The highest point is the Lerbjerg, rising proudly to over 400 ft. In addition to the typically Danish beech-woods, birches and firs are also found in this area.

52. The Danish landscape is marked almost everywhere by glacial deposits, in contrast to the Scandinavian peninsula proper, where the primeval rock is a much more prominent feature. Strata of older rock appear on the surface only in very few places in Denmark, including Stevns Klint, on the east coast of Zealand (pl. 59) and the island of MØEN. Even here it is 'only' cretaceous rock, a comparatively recent formation, which makes the east coast of this island, where the cliffs rise in some places to a height of over 400 ft., one of the most singular and picturesque stretches of the Danish coast.

53. ODENSE is the capital of the island of Funen and, with its population of about 125,000, is Denmark's third largest city after Copenhagen and Århus. Odense is one of the oldest towns in the north and its name recalls the god Odin, whose shrine once stood on this spot. From 1020 until the Reformation in 1527 it was a bishopric. The Gothic church of St Canute, a brick edifice built between 1250 and 1350, is the most important architectural monument of the city's past. In contrast to other Danish towns with a great past, such as Ribe (pl. 64) or Roskilde (pl. 47) which under the influence of the rise of Copenhagen sank to merely local importance, modern Odense has developed into an important industrial and commercial centre, not least because of its excellent situation on trade and communication routes in the centre of the island. Although by Danish standards it is regarded as an inland town, Odense possesses one of the most important ports in the country and since 1804 has been linked with the Odense Fjord by a 5-mile-long canal. In a small, unpretentious house in the old town (pl. 53), Hans Christian Andersen was born on 2 April 1805.

54. Den Gamle By (the old town), the open-air museum of ÅRHUS (pls. 65, 66), unlike most other Scandinavian open-air museums, is not devoted to country life, but to town life in the sixteenth and seventeenth centuries. More than fifty houses and public buildings characteristic of old Danish towns have been assembled since the founding of the museum in 1914 and formed into a model town. The entire interior furnishings and fittings illustrate middle-class town life, the history of the crafts and the folklore of east Jutland.

55. The reforming efforts of the Cistercian order extended in the twelfth century towards the north. LØGUM-KLOSTER in south Jutland is a Cistercian foundation (1177). The brick-built monastery church, with its Romanesque and Gothic features, dates from about 1300. In the background on the right are the stairs leading to the former monks' dormitory.

56 In the high standard of craftsmanship and the great pictorial value of Danish church art of the early Middle Ages the force and vitality of the Viking days can still be sensed. The products of the metal-workers of Jutland were eagerly sought after, even abroad. A number of oaken altars faced with finely wrought and gilded copper have been preserved, among them this GOLD ALTAR FROM SALE (Jutland), dating from the second half of the twelfth or the early thirteenth century.

57 The miniature palace of BERRITSGÅRD near Sakskøbing on Lolland was built in 1586 for Elizabeth Friis.

58 The first half of the sixteenth century in Denmark was a time of great internal strife. During a peasant uprising in 1534 the manor house of Solling (north Jutland) was burnt down; in its place was built the stronghold of SPØTTRUP, defended by a double moat and a wall. Spøttrup was a so-called 'ox-farm', that is to say a nobleman's estate on which the chief activity was the raising of oxen for export.

59 In the south-east of Zealand the cliffs of STEVNS KLINT stretch for some 10 miles at an average height of 130 ft. Unlike that on the island of Møen, the chalk here is overlaid with younger limestone strata. The hollow fluting action of the breakers can be clearly seen along the lower part of the overhanging limestone cliffs. The description of the chalk cliffs of Stevns Klint, written by Søren Abildgaard (1708–91), was one of the first pieces of scientific research in mineralogy to be carried out in Denmark.

60 The lively industrial and commercial town of RANDERS, Denmark's fifth largest town (pop. 57,000) is situated in Jutland, north-west of Århus, where the Gudenå flows into the Randers Fjord. The Gudenå is Denmark's longest river (75 miles). The Town Hall (pl. 60) dates from 1778.

61 Denmark is usually thought of as primarily agricultural country. In fact today only about 25 per cent of the inhabitants are engaged in agriculture as against more than one-third in industry. The chief exports, however, are still high-quality agricultural products, chiefly bacon, butter, cheese, eggs and tinned goods. Danish agriculture is characterized by medium-sized farms of 25 to 75 acres. The large manorial farms have almost disappeared, having been divided up for small farming. Most of Denmark is under cultivation, 74 per cent being pasture-land and more than 44 per cent of the cultivated area devoted to cereal crops. Co-operatives are highly developed and widespread in all sectors. This photograph shows a farm at ROSKILDE on Zealand.

62 ÅLBORG (pop. c. 95,000; with Nørresundby c. 116,000) is in Jutland on the south bank of the Lim Fjord which joins the North Sea and the Kattegat. The town has an old tradition of industry and commerce and was early one of the largest centres for trade with Norway.

On the Lindholm hills near Ålborg is the largest excavation site in Denmark. Between 1952 and 1958 a burial place used in the early Stone Age and in Viking days was uncovered, together with the remains of an eleventh-century settlement. These stone ship-building stocks from Viking times are among the most 'modern' finds.

63 This great rune stone, which lies today with another (seen in the background) in what is now the cemetery at Jelling near VEJLE (east Jutland) was erected by Harald Bluetooth about the year 985. It has been called Denmark's 'baptismal stone' on account of its inscription: 'King Harald had these mounds set up for Gorm his father and Tyre his mother, that Harald who conquered the whole of Denmark and Norway and made the Danes Christians'. The stone, whose inscription belongs to the later series of runes (cf. pl. 101) is richly ornamented and was certainly originally brightly painted. The two hidden sides bear two main figures cut into the stone in low relief: a Christ with a halo, surrounded by ornamental scroll-work and a lion killing a serpent. Runes, especially those cut in stone, are the oldest monuments of the Nordic languages. The main period for runic inscriptions was from 900 to 1050, but considerably earlier and considerably later ones are known. Denmark has altogether about 600.

64 RIBE (pop. 7,700), on the banks of the River Ribe in the marshes of south-west Jutland, was, with Roskilde (pl. 48), one of the most important towns in Denmark in the Middle Ages. Ribe is thought to be the oldest town in the country if not in the whole of Scandinavia. A bishopric since 948, this town, whose Cathedral School is the oldest in Denmark (built in 1145), has long been and remained an intellectual centre, though its economic importance has not been maintained in modern times.

The Cathedral, with those of Lund (pl. 78) and Viborg, is one of the few large Romanesque buildings in Scandinavia. Like the other two, the Cathedral of Ribe shows Lombard influences which reached the north by way of the Rhenish cathedrals, especially Speyer. In Ribe even the stone is imported Rhenish volcanic limestone. The basilica with its three naves was built on the site of an older church dedicated to St Ansgar, 'the Apostle of the North'. It was begun in the early twelfth century and completed for the most part by the end of the century. The larger of the two western towers was built later, towards the middle of the thirteenth century, by the townspeople partly for defence purposes.

65–6 ÅRHUS, on the Kattegat, the capital of Jutland, is with its 165,000 inhabitants the second largest Danish city. At times in the sixteenth and seventeenth centuries Århus had a larger population than Copenhagen. Its ideal position for trade on the Kattegat accounts for its rise as an important industrial and commercial centre, which in many sectors is second only to Copenhagen. In spite of its great age—the town received its charter in 1441—Århus gives the impression of a new, young, energetic community.

65. The UNIVERSITY of Århus is a modern founda‐ tion. Although the establishment of a second university near Copenhagen was many times mooted in past centuries, nothing was actually done until 1928, when part of a Faculty of Philosophy was opened—entirely with private and municipal funds, without any support from the Danish Government. Today the University of Århus is complete with five Faculties. The main building (pl. 65), designed by the architect C. F. Møller, was begun in 1933, but was not inaugurated until 1946—the still unfinished structure having suffered war‐damage during the intervening period.

66. The PORT of Århus is the second largest in Denmark. Its vast docks, protected from the storms of the Kattegat by the peninsula of Djursland to the north‐east, are fitted out with the latest modern equipment (about 8 miles of wharves).

67 VESTERHAUSBAD is the largest bathing resort on the island of Fanø (cf. pl. 20). The dunes with their sparse covering of grass stretch almost the whole way along the coast of west Jutland from Esbjerg, the only important port, up to Skagen (cf. pl. 39).

68 FISHERIES and their associated industries, particularly processing, are an important branch of the Danish economy. The natural conditions—a long coastline and abundantly stocked waters—are favourable to Danish fisheries, which have expanded especially rapidly since the introduction of modern technical aids. The most important fishing grounds are the North Sea and the Skagerrak (chiefly herring, plaice, cod, sole—in 1957 a total of 230,000 tons). Although important, fishing in the Kattegat, the Belts, the Sound, the Baltic and the fjords is less productive.

Every summer tunny‐fish seek out Danish waters, in very large numbers in recent years. Itself a hunter, the tunny is hunted in turn by professional fishermen and sportsmen (pl. 68); it feeds on the shoals of fish in the Sound and the Belts.

69 The north coast of the island of BORNHOLM is the only part of Denmark where the primeval rock—granite and gneiss—appears on the surface and forms the landscape. Everywhere else in Denmark it has been proved by boring to lie far below the younger strata, which are chiefly of chalk and limestone (cf. pls. 52, 59). In the area between the primeval rock of Sweden and Denmark's sedimentary rock, great blocks (*Horste*) were raised up in the Tertiary era, while others subsided. Bornholm is one of the former. At the north end of the island the rocky subsoil forms a wild, indented coast with cliffs and rocky islands, clefts and caves. Although geologically and geographically it belongs to the Scandinavian peninsula, politically Bornholm (223 sq. miles) has been part of Denmark since 1522. The 400‐year tutelage of the bishops of Lund (Danish until 1658) and the Danish kings was interrupted only briefly in the middle of the seventeenth century by Swedish occupation in the war with Sweden. The island is well situated for trade and communications; its inhabitants (*c.* 50,000) are mainly engaged in fishing and agriculture, and to some small extent in stone quarrying. Bornholm's four well‐preserved medieval round churches (cf. pl. 50) make it of marked architectural interest.

SWEDEN

Plates 70–133

Sweden, lying between latitude 55° and 69° north and between longitude 10° and 24° east and comprising the eastern and southern part of the Scandinavian peninsula, is one of Europe's largest countries. Of its 173,206 sq. miles, 25,100 sq. miles or 15 per cent lie north of the Arctic Circle, 14,900 sq. miles consist of water, and 69,900 sq. miles are wooded. The greatest width of the peninsula is about 300 miles. Of its seven and a half million inhabitants, some 70 per cent live today in the towns and thickly settled areas (average population density: 44 per sq. mile).

Sweden forms the core of the primeval rock formation that characterizes Scandinavia: granite and gneiss are its main geological components. The fertile sandstone and limestone regions of central and southern Sweden, on the other hand, are due to marine deposits in the Cambrian and Silurian periods, while Skåne, in the extreme south, is formed, like Denmark, of layers of chalk of much more recent date.

During the Ice Age, Sweden was entirely covered by ice-floes which, on retreating, left moraine deposits of an average depth of 13 to 16 ft. over three-quarters of the country.

Apart from the mountainous area in the north and west, the Fjäll country, the main natural regions are: the interior of northern Sweden, or 'Norrland', east and south-east of the Fjäll chain, with its vast forests and numerous rivers; the Norrland coast, with Sweden's only fjords, the central Highlands with the great lakes of Väner, Vätter and Mälar, and lastly the southern Highlands (Småland) with its bordering regions (the Islands of Gotland and Öland, the coastal plains of Kalmar and Halland, and Skåne).

Numerous archaeological finds indicate that Sweden was settled in prehistoric times. In the centuries following the great migrations and above all during the Viking Age, settlers pushed far into Russia (founding Novgorod in 862) bringing extensive trade in their train. Sweden was not fully Christianized until after the end of the tenth century. In the thirteenth century, Finland was subjugated and converted to Christianity. The modern Swedish State dates back to Gustav Vasa who in 1523 freed the country from union with Denmark and created a national State with a hereditary monarchy. His grandson, Gustav II Adolf, laid the foundations of Sweden's power in the seventeenth century, but, owing to losses in the wars of the late seventeenth and early eighteenth century, it was of short duration. In 1809, Finland was lost to Russia. Norway was attached to the Swedish crown from 1814 to 1905.

70-1 Opposite Copenhagen, on the Swedish side, at the southern exit of the Sound lies MALMÖ, the capital of the province of Skåne and Sweden's third largest town (pop. *c.* 125,000). Malmö is mentioned in the chronicles for the first time towards the end of the twelfth century and the first establishment of the present town dates from 1275. Malmö, like the rest of the province of Skåne, was Danish until it passed to Sweden by the Peace of Roskilde in 1658. It owes its rapid rise as an important and prosperous trading centre in the sixteenth century to the growing importance of herring fishing in the Sound. Its port, today Sweden's largest artificial harbour, with the most considerable import traffic in the country, was not built until 1775. Pl. 71 shows the view from the western side of the inner harbour towards the town; on the right is St Peter's Church. With Greater Stockholm and Greater Göteborg, Malmö-Hälsingborg is one of Sweden's three most densely populated and most industrialized areas. Ninety per cent of the Swedish ship-building industry is concentrated on the west coast (pl. 70) at Malmö, Göteborg, Uddevalla, Hälsingborg and Landskrona. With a gross tonnage of 864,000 coming off the stocks (1959), Sweden is the fourth ship-building nation of the world.

72-4 GÖTEBORG (pop. 400,000) was founded by Gustav Adolf. In 1620 he ordered the town to be built at the mouth of the Götaälv, on the site of the older settlement of Nya Lödöse, and settled Dutch, Scottish and German immigrants there. The remains of a network of canals on the Dutch model are still to be seen. The purpose of the town, namely to give Sweden a good outlet to the North Sea at a time when almost all the southern part of the country was still under Danish rule, has been, as history shows, amply fulfilled. Göteborg is today Sweden's most important port for exports (pl. 72) and, after Stockholm, the country's largest industrial city. Göteborg's importance increased rapidly at the beginning of the nineteenth century, during the Continental blockade, when it became the principal port for English trade with Northern Europe. Its institutes for higher education and museums also make Göteborg the cultural centre for south-west Sweden.

Modern Swedish architecture has found good solutions in Göteborg for the most varied types of building. Examples of this are the Crematorium of the Kviberg cemetery, with the two chapels of St Olof and St Sigfrid (pl. 73, built in 1951 and 1958) and the new covered swimming pool (pl. 74).

75 HÄLSINGBORG, with a population of some 77,000, is Sweden's fifth largest town. It is situated at the narrowest part of the Sound, less than 3 miles from the Danish town of Helsingør (pl. 42), with which it is linked by the busiest of the ferry services between the two countries. Hälsingborg is an ancient town, mentioned in chronicles as early as the tenth century. It rose to its present importance only when the dues levied on shipping in the Sound by the Danish kings were

abolished in 1857. The restaurant 'The Parapets' at the harbour entrance (pl. 75) was built for an exhibition in 1955.

76 Malmö, Hälsingborg and LANDSKRONA are the three largest towns on the Swedish side of the Sound, and the focal points of the highly industrialized and thickly populated region of western Skåne. The metal industry, represented by numerous firms, some of them highly specialized, producing a wide range of manu-factured goods, is one of the most important sectors of the economy, especially in southern Sweden. More than 30 per cent of Swedish industrial manpower (*c.* 200,000) is employed in the metal industry, which produces more than a quarter, by value, of Swedish exports.

77 The castle of KALMAR on the south coast, opposite the island of Öland, evokes one of the most important events in Scandinavian history. After prolonged negotiations, the Kalmar Union was concluded here in 1397, uniting Denmark, Norway with its Atlantic islands, and Sweden, which then embraced a large part of Finland, under Queen Margrete of Denmark.

The majestic castle, with its four wings and five towers, was built in the twelfth century, enlarged in the sixteenth century and restored in the nineteenth century.

78 Besides Kalmar, the town of LUND (pop. 40,000) in Skåne, north-west of Malmö also evokes historic memories. Like most of southern Sweden, Lund, the 'Metropolis Daniae', belonged to Denmark until 1658. In the Middle Ages it was for long the largest town in Scandinavia, but was burnt down by the Swedes in the war of 1452 and thereafter never regained its influence. The University of Lund was founded by Charles XI in 1666, after the union with Sweden.

The Cathedral, the crypt of which is shown here, is, with those of Ribe and Viborg (cf. pl. 64), one of the three important Romanesque cathedrals in Scandinavia. Begun about 1080 by St Canute, and consecrated in 1145, this edifice, in which influences of the Rhenish and northern Italian church architecture of the day combine, is the oldest metropolitan church of the north.

79 A third historic centre in southern Sweden in addition to Kalmar and Lund is Vadstena on the east shore of Lake Vätter. The Order of St Bridget founded its first convent here in 1383—a combined monastery and convent in which monks and nuns worked and prayed together, though strictly segregated. Around this foundation the present town grew up. From Vadstena, the Order of St Bridget spread throughout Europe and established some eighty monasteries.

Gustav Vasa built the Palace of VADSTENA (pl. 79) about 1545. It is one of Sweden's finest Renaissance buildings.

80 Sweden has only one canal system of any significance, the GÖTAKANAL, which runs from the North Sea to the Baltic by way of Lakes Vätter and Väner (Sweden's two largest lakes) and the Götaälv. Its terminal points are Stockholm and Göteborg, and its total length about 335 miles. The idea of connecting the Baltic with Lake Vätter was put forward as early as the seventeenth century, and work was actually started in the early eighteenth century. However, it was not completed until the beginning of the nineteenth century, by which time the technique of lock con-struction had been completely mastered. The western end of the canal was opened in 1822 and the eastern end in 1832. At some points it runs as high as 298 ft. above sea-level; to control this gradient, a positive stairway of locks had to be built, as our photograph shows.

81 STRÄNGNÄS (pop. *c.* 8,500) is an idyllic peaceful town on the southern shore of Lake Mälar, quite undisturbed as yet by the throbbing life and spreading tentacles of Stockholm, which sprawls at the eastern end of the same lake. From the twelfth century onwards, the bishop, whose diocese also included the capital, had his seat here. This view of the town and the lake was taken from the tower of the cathedral, a thirteenth-century building which has been considerably altered at later periods.

82-3 BOHUSLÄN (1,740 sq. miles), the province which includes Göteborg, is the westernmost part of Sweden. It takes its name from the fortress of Bohus, built in 1310 by King Håkon of Norway on an island in the Nordre Älv. The primeval rock, worn down by the glaciers of the Ice Age, rises to the surface on the mainland and is even more in evidence on the count-less rocky islands that fringe the jagged coast (pl. 83). Here, as along the east coast near Stockholm and on the Norwegian coast, the belt of rock islets was created when the level of the mainland rose as a result of the withdrawal of the ice—a process which is not yet concluded.

84-5 GOTLAND is the largest of the Baltic islands (1,220 sq. miles, pop. 56,000). In contrast to the mainland of Sweden, which consists chiefly of primeval rock, Gotland is a mass of Silurian calcareous formations (average height 99-164 ft.), falling in vertical cliffs to the sea. Gotland's great period was in the twelfth to fourteenth centuries, when it controlled the Baltic trade and when the merchants of Visby, its capital, were partners in the Hansa with those of Lübeck—the city which ultimately outmatched Visby. In 1361, Visby was destroyed by the Danish King Valdemar Atterdag, after which the town, and Gotland itself, became mere pawns in the endless match played between the Danes, Germans, Swedes and Russians.

The buildings surviving from Visby's period of prosperity are only a fraction of those it once possessed, but even so they are sufficiently impressive, as the so-called OLD APOTHECARY'S SHOP (pl. 84), for example, indicates. The CITY WALLS (pl. 85) have no parallel elsewhere in Sweden; they were built towards the end of the thirteenth century, embodying earlier fortifications constructed of limestone. The towers, placed at regular distances along the wall, rise to a height of from 50—66 ft. and thirty-eight of them still survive.

86 ÖLAND (519 sq. miles; pop. c. 27,000) lies off the southern coast of Sweden, divided from the mainland by the narrow Kalmar Sound. Like Gotland, it is a mass of calcareous rock; like Gotland too, it has proved to be a treasure-house of relics of prehistoric and early historical times. Its western coast rises steeply out of the sea to a height of 130–154 ft., from which the land slopes gradually eastwards in a declining plateau. Only one narrow strip is cultivable and comparatively densely populated. The only town of any size is Borgholm (pop. 2,500). Borgholm Castle (pl. 86) dates from the thirteenth century. It was renovated in 1572 and destroyed by fire in 1806, since when it has held the reputation of being Sweden's largest ruined castle.

87 GOTSKA SANDÖN, a little island in the Baltic, north of Gotland, consists chiefly of sand. It is kept as a nature reserve and is unpopulated except by the crew of its lighthouse.

88 The church at ROGSLÖSA, at Östergötland, on the eastern shore of Lake Vätter, is one of the many medieval country churches in Sweden where beautiful works of art form part of the structure. Rogslösa's great feature is its twelfth-century iron-studded door, on which St Michael the Archangel, a hunting scene and other themes are depicted. The church itself was built in the twelfth century and considerably transformed in the thirteenth century, under Cistercian influence.

89 SIGTUNA (pop. 14,000) is situated between Stockholm and Uppsala, on an arm of Lake Mälar. It was founded by King Olov Erikson in the early eleventh century and is the oldest town in Sweden to have preserved its original plan, together with a good number of the buildings erected after its destruction by the Estonians in 1187. In the provinces of Västergötland and Östergötland and on the island of Gotland, the local building materials were sandstone and limestone so that many handsome churches of hewn stone were erected; whereas those round Lake Mälar are characterized by cyclopean granite masonry which is extremely impressive, particularly in the ruins of Sigtuna.

St Per, the church in this picture, was built about the year 1100.

90 A regatta in STORA VÄRTAN BAY, near Stockholm, which lies between Djursholm and the Rydbo Peninsula.

91-104 STOCKHOLM, the capital of Sweden, stands at the eastern end of Lake Mälar, where the inland waters flow into the Baltic in the Bay of Saltsjön. It thus occupies a good strategic position at the entrance to the Gulf of Bothnia, protected by a deep belt of rocky islets. Stockholm was founded in 1252 by the Imperial Administrator Birger Jarl, with the royal castle as its central point. At first only the islands now known as Staden, Helgeandsholmen and Riddarholmen were built up and fortified; not until much later did a permanent settlement come into existence on the mainland. The first royal coronation took place at Stockholm in 1336.

During the period of the Kalmar Union Stockholm dwindled, largely as a result of the unfavourable economic repercussions of the struggle between Denmark and the Hansa. But under the Vasa dynasty, and more especially with the inception of Sweden's period as a great Power towards the middle of the seventeenth century, the town made rapid progress. By 1700 it had become a spiritual, intellectual and artistic centre, with 75,000 inhabitants—whereas about the year 1630 the population had numbered only 8,000. After so long remaining huddled round its original core, the town had begun to spread rapidly over the mainland. Stockholm now has a population of 780,000 (1,200,000 for Greater Stockholm) and one of its most distinctive features is its spacious ground-plan.

91. On 10 August 1628 the *Vasa*, King Gustav Adolf's new 1,400-ton flagship, was hit by a squall in Stockholm harbour with all sails set, and sank with all hands.

Attempts were made soon afterwards to refloat her but they failed, and only a few of the guns were recovered. After this the matter was dismissed and the position of the wreck forgotten until it was rediscovered in 1956. The salvage operations scored their first triumph on 24 April 1961, when the ship, which had originally lain in about 115 ft. of water, was brought to the surface. The *Vasa* is the oldest vessel of certain identity in the world. Our picture shows her docked in a concrete pontoon which will probably constitute the floor of the future *Vasa* Museum.

92–3. At the north-east corner of Staden island, the oldest part of the city, stands the ROYAL PALACE, the construction of which was begun by Charles XII and his architect, Nicodemus Tessin the Elder (1654–1728) in 1697, after the original castle on the same site had been destroyed by fire. Progress was interrupted for many years because Charles XII's wars had drained the treasury dry, and not until the middle of the eighteenth century was the construction completed, by the son of the architect. It is a magnificent, nobly proportioned building standing four-square round a central court-yard, with two lower wings on the north side.

Every Wednesday the ceremony of Changing the Guard takes place in the outer courtyard and here, as at Copenhagen, it is a popular spectacle.

94. Behind the palace is the STORKYRKA (Great Church), the oldest parish church in Stockholm, where every Swedish monarch has been crowned since the fifteenth century. Its oldest parts date from the thirteenth century; the façade was given a baroque aspect in 1736–43 (see pl. 98).

The most impressive feature of the decoration is the large, painted wooden statue of St George and the Dragon, by the wood-carver of Lübeck, Bernt Notke. This was presented to the church in 1489 by the Imperial Administrator, Sten Sture the Elder, in memory of his victory over the Danes on the Brunke-berg, outside Stockholm, in 1471.

95. Riksdaghuset, the HOUSES OF PARLIAMENT, built in 1898–1904 to the design of Aron Johansson.

Sweden has a long-standing parliamentary tradition, the people's representatives having met for the first time at Arboga in the year 1435. In 1866 the two-chamber system was introduced. The 151 members of the Upper House are elected for an eight-year period by the provincial parliaments and the Senates of the six large cities, while the 251 deputies in the Lower House are elected by direct and universal suffrage every four years.

96. SLUSSEN, the 'Lock', is the busiest traffic centre in Stockholm. The first lock was constructed here in 1637 to correct the difference in level between Lake Mälar

and the Baltic, which meet at this point. The ingenious arrangement seen in the foreground, which enables vehicles to be guided in the right direction at three different levels without a crossing, was introduced in 1936 and illustrates the far-sighted town and traffic planning characteristic of Stockholm. Opposite Slussen is the southern end of Staden Island and, on the extreme left, Riddarholmen (cf. separate view, pl. 98).

97. At the southernmost tip of the large island of Kungsholmen stands Stockholm's NEW TOWN HALL (Stadshuset), a commanding structure, visible from a great distance. In the architecture of the first quarter of our century it would be difficult to find another public building where traditional forms are so convincingly combined with a modern attitude towards architecture, so entirely free from eclectic romanticism. This Town Hall was built between 1911 and 1923 to the design of Ragnar Östberg, and the best Swedish artists of the day contributed to its interior decoration (see also pl. 98).

98. The view from Stadshuset tower (over 347 ft. high) is one of the most impressive city panoramas in the world.

The small island of RIDDARHOLMEN is seen in the foreground, with the bridges which link it to Staden. It is dominated by the cast-iron spire of the Riddar-holm Church, which was set in place in 1840. Every Swedish king since Gustav Adolf has been buried in this church, the greater part of which, despite many changes and much restoration, dates from the period of its foundation (late thirteenth century). The spire seen in the middle of the picture is that of the Tyska Kyrka (German Church), built by German merchants in 1636–42 (see also pl. 96, right). To the left is the tower of the Storkyrka (see pl. 94). The building in the left foreground, with the two pavilions in front of it, is the Riddarhuset, in which the assembly of the Swedish peers used to meet until 1866; it is perhaps the finest seventeenth-century building in Stockholm. On the extreme right of the picture we see Slussen (cf. pl. 96).

99. Stockholm's town-planning is bold and has an eye to the future. In the city itself a new business quarter is being constructed and an underground railway network is coming into operation; satellite towns are rising on the outskirts.

Vällingby, in north-west Stockholm, was designed as a town in its own right. It is not intended to be a 'dormitory town', but a community with its own centre of gravity, its own places of work and all the equipment of a modern town, which will ease the pressure on Stockholm to a really appreciable extent. This aim has been summed up in the formula A-B-C (*Arbeit-Behausing-Centrum*—Work and Residential Centre).

Farsta, the counterpart of Vällingby on the south side of Stockholm, is designed for a population of 70,000.

100. Carl Milles (1875–1955) is regarded as the most important Swedish sculptor of the twentieth century, and his ORPHEUS GROUP outside the Stockholm Concert Hall (see colour-plate VII) as a masterpiece of modern Swedish sculpture. In his old age he arranged some of his own works, with statues he had collected on his travels, in the terraced garden of his house in Stockholm which he opened to the public. The statues, on their slender pillars, the design of the gardens, with their Italianate atmosphere and the view of Stockholm across the water give the place a unique charm, quite different from the massive effect of the Vigeland Park at Oslo (see pls. 140–3).

101–4 Stockholm's famous open-air museum of folk art is called SKANSEN ('the small redoubt'), in reference to the fortifications that formerly occupied this eminence on Djurgaden Island. It has inspired many similar projects in other countries, particularly in Scandinavia (cf. pls. 38, 54, 146, 147).

The original idea of such a museum was put forward by Arthur Hazelius (1833–1901), the ethnographer, art historian, teacher and patriot, and backed by the enthusiastic appreciation of the old Swedish peasant culture which swept through the country towards the end of the nineteenth century. Skansen was opened on 31 August 1891 as an outdoor department of the Scandinavian Museum, which stands just outside the park.

The original purpose was to rescue ancient Swedish monuments from the danger of destruction, but the work was gradually extended to present an overall view of the social life of every class and condition of the Swedish population in the last four hundred years.

101. All the RUNE STONES brought to Skansen date from the eleventh century A.D. and thus bear engravings of the 'newer runic series', an alphabet of sixteen signs, developed from the original twenty-four signs by a process of simplification. The lavish decoration which is also to be seen on the stone in our photograph, indicates that it comes from the province of Uppland, the richest source of rune-stones in the Germanic world, where nearly 1,000 stones have been found.

102. The RAVLUNDA farmhouse was brought to Skansen from the parish of Ravlunda, near Albo, in southern Skåne. It offers a typical example of peasant architecture in the plains of Skåne—built round the four sides of an almost square, enclosed yard, with the living-quarters (shown in the photograph) joined to the farm buildings.

103. The KYRKHULT house was moved to Skansen from Kyrkhult in western Blekinge (South Sweden). On festive occasions the walls and ceilings of the rooms used to be hung with the embroidered or woven tapestries characteristic of this region. Our picture shows one such hanging, which depicts a wedding scene.

104. This storehouse from BJÖRKVIST follows the style of a barn belonging to a manor-house in Östergötland. Built of thick beams, it consists of three storeys without partitions; a covered balcony entirely surrounds the first floor. Food used to be stored on the ground floor and clothes on the first floor.

105–7 DROTTNINGHOLM CASTLE, which stands on an island in Lake Mälar, is the summer residence of the royal family. It was begun in 1661 to the design of N. Tessin the Elder, in the French style, and completed by his son, who built the palace at Stockholm.

106, 107. The Drottningholm THEATRE (erected in 1764–6 on the site of an earlier playhouse) is outstanding among the surviving eighteenth-century court theatres, for not only is its auditorium intact, but its original stage machinery is still in working order and it has thirty complete sets of scenery dating from the time when it was built. Since 1922 it has been in use again, for summer performances.

108 LUCIADAGEN, the 13 December, is celebrated all over Sweden as the survival, or in some cases the revival, of an old pagan custom. Coming after what was originally believed to be the longest night of the year, it greets the beginning of the longer days, symbolized by 'Lucia's' bridal crown of lights. Every house, village and town has its own Lucia, who walks round it with her followers offering coffee and cakes.

109 Christmas service in the church at DANDERYD in central Sweden.

Almost all Swedes—some 98 per cent of the population—are Protestants, though the Swedish Church is now disestablished and freedom of religion is guaranteed by the law. The proportion is much the same in the other Scandinavian countries. The Reformation reached the Nordic countries chiefly between 1530 and 1540. The State—the King, the Government and the Parliament—still has a considerable say in Church affairs in Sweden.

110-12 UPPSALA (pop. 77,000) is Sweden's most ancient political and cultural centre. The Uppsala kings laid the foundation of the Swedish Empire 1,200 years ago by uniting a number of small States. On the site of the present city there was originally only Östra Aros (the 'eastern estuary'), market and harbour of Gamla Uppsala—the old royal and religious city of pagan times, where the Christian bishops later established their seat (in 1164; it was moved to Östra Aros in 1270). For a long time Uppsala was the scene of the coronation and one of the most important towns in Sweden, but in 1702 there was an outbreak of fire which almost completely destroyed it.

The CATHEDRAL, begun in the thirteenth century, in the northern French style, and consecrated in 1435 (pl. 110), is the finest Gothic building in the country. Several kings are buried there, including Gustav Vasa. The University, still the largest in Sweden, was founded in 1447.

One of the high spots in the year for students is WALPURGIS NIGHT, 30 April, when they assemble to greet the return of spring with songs (pl. 110). Another occasion which is celebrated with great exuberance is the conclusion of the school-leaving examinations, when the young Swedes exchange their old school caps for the white cap of the student (pl. 111).

112. GAMLA UPPSALA (Old Uppsala) was one of the last surviving strongholds of paganism in Sweden— a country to which Christianity came late in any case— and held out until about 1100. The most impressive vestiges of paganism are the three royal barrows, dating from about 450-550, in which three kings of the Svear lie buried.

113-14 VÄRMLAND is the region of the great manor-houses. One of the most celebrated of these is Rottneros Hergård, the Ekeby of Selma Lagerlöf's *Gösta Berling*, a beautiful place visited by thousands of people every year. Mårbacka, not far away, was Selma Lagerlöf's own home, where she spent part of her life.

115 MORA, in Dalarna (pop. c. 13,000) is the general name for several neighbouring villages at the north-west end of Lake Siljan. Anders Zorn (1860-1920), Sweden's leading impressionist painter, came from

Mora. The traditional-style farmhouse where he lived, together with his studio, is kept in its original condition as a memorial to him. Of all Swedish provinces, Dalarna is the most faithful to tradition; the old peasant culture, with its manners and customs, is more deeply rooted here than anywhere else.

116 The peasant families living beside LAKE SILJAN join together on Sundays to take the 'Church boat' to morning service.

117 The province of Uppland, North of Stockholm, has a wealth of medieval country churches. ROSLAGSBRO Church was built in the thirteenth century and the triumphal cross (centre of picture) dates from the same period. The frescoes were added later (1471).

118 Albertus Pictor, the great Swedish painter of the late Middle Ages, did not do his finest work in Stockholm, where he lived, but in a number of village churches in central Sweden (from about 1470-90). The frescoes in TÄBY church are among his masterpieces.

119 Like other countries with a long-standing cultural tradition, Sweden developed its PAPER INDUSTRY at an early period. When wood-pulp became the chief raw material for paper-making, the country's wealth of timber developed this into an important branch of the economic system. The industry is concentrated in south and central Sweden, particularly in Värmland, north-west of Lake Väner, and along the Götaälv.

120 Modern Swedish handicrafts have won international fame—textiles, furniture, metal-work, and above all, glass. The high artistic and technical quality of these products is based on ancient traditions of peasant craftsmanship. As early as the middle of the sixteenth century, Stockholm was producing valuable glassware. Today Sweden has over fifty glass furnaces, the most celebrated being Kosta, Orrefors and Strömbergshyttan in Småland.

121 The Swedish mining industry is principally located in three districts—the Bergslagen region in central Sweden, where valuable iron ores are mined to meet the needs of the Swedish iron and steel industry, the iron mines in north Norrland (cf. pl. 132) and the large group of non-ferrous metal mines—which chiefly produce copper—along the lower course of the Skellefte Älv and on the Gulf of Bothnia in North Sweden. Copper is no longer produced from the cele-brated Falun mine, which for 650 years yielded more

copper than any other mine in the world; the Sala silvermines, too, have been closed since 1920.

In the middle of the eighteenth century Sweden was producing some 40 per cent of the world's iron ore. Her present annual output of 20 million tons still represents something over 3 per cent. From 80 to 90 per cent of this is exported.

122 This large factory at KARLSHAMN in the province of Blekinge, south-east Sweden, produces more vegetable oils and fats than any other in the country.

123 Swedish NORRLAND, the district to the north of the Dalälv, with its huge forests, lakes, tumultuous rivers and mountains, attracted little or no attention until comparatively recent times.

Even Linnaeus (1707–78) wrote of it in his *Iter Lapponicum* that 'The priests need not be at pains to describe the horrors of Hell; this place is far worse'. Sweden did not begin to pay serious attention to Norrland until after 1809, when Finland was lost to Russia. Nowadays its wealth of timber, its minerals and its water power make it an important factor in the country's economic life (cf. pls. 124–6, 132).

124–6 Sweden's forests are her chief natural wealth and therefore of the greatest importance to her economy. They supply the raw material for about 25 per cent of the country's industrial production and 40 per cent of its exports. At the height of the season, in winter, some 300,000 men are employed as woodcutters and loggers.

127 SÖRLEVIK, a bay on the Gulf of Bothnia in the north Swedish province of Ångermanland.

128 UNDERSVIK, in the province of Hälsingland, north Sweden. Forest-clad mountain ranges and mighty rivers, with arable land in the river valleys, are the characteristic features of the provinces round the Gulf of Bothnia. In the background is the Öresjön range.

129 HUDIKSVALL (pop. *c*. 12,500) is one of Norrland's oldest towns, founded in 1582. It lies on the Gulf of Bothnia, and has a harbour and a timber industry. Hudiksvall is divided from north to south by the Sund Canal, lined with old beach huts, which connects the two bays on which the town is built.

130 ÅNGERMANLAND, a province lying along the lower course of the Ångermanälv (*c*. 7,722 sq. miles, capital Härnosänd) is a mountainous region of great scenic beauty, with precipitous-sided fjords running into the Gulf of Bothnia.

131 The ÅNGERMANÄLV (cf. pl. 133) in north Sweden rises in Norway and flows south-eastwards, parallel to many other rivers in central and north Sweden, into the Gulf of Bothnia, by which time it has become a wide stream and forms a fertile delta. Its total length is about 270 miles, and it is navigable for some 60 miles. The Ångermanälv is one of the principal waterways for the transport of timber (cf. pls. 124, 125). The big bridge near Kramfors was constructed in 1938–41.

132 The iron-mining town of KIRUNA in northern Lapland (pop. *c*. 27,000) is Sweden's most northerly town, founded in 1890. The name covers a number of scattered settlements built round different iron-mines, and the whole district constitutes the largest township in the world (*c*. 5,406 sq. miles). The production of iron ore in north Sweden, chiefly at Kiruna and Gällivare, is the most considerable in the whole country. Unlike the deposits in central Sweden, the northern ore lies at or immediately below the surface so that open-cast mining is possible in places. It is estimated that Kiruna's reserves of ore—the iron content of which ranges from 60–70 per cent—amount to about a thousand million tons. Most of the exported ore (some 12 million tons a year) is conveyed over the Lapland railway to Narvik (see pl. 179) and shipped from there.

133 The HARRFORSEN Falls on the Ångermanälv are now diverted and controlled, but in summer, during the tourist season, the stream is released into its original bed again.

NORWAY
Plates 134–193

Norway lies between latitude 57° and 71° north and between longitude 4° and 31° east. It is bordered on the north by the Arctic Ocean, on the west by the Atlantic Ocean and the North Sea, and on the south by the Skagerrak, and has land frontiers with Sweden and the USSR. It covers an area of 125,096 sq. miles and measures 1,056 miles from north to south at its greatest extent. Over a third of the country lies north of the 65th parallel. Its outlying territories include Spitsbergen, Bear Island, Jan Mayen, Bouvet Island, Peter I Island and Queen Maud Land in the Antarctic.

Geologically speaking, Norway occupies the western edge of the great basement complex of Fennoskandia. The Scandinavian mountain chain, which in Sweden slopes fairly gradually eastward, falls in precipices to the sea along much of the Norwegian coast (the coastline is slightly over 2,000 miles long); here, and beside the deep inland fjords cut out by the glaciers of the Ice Age, there is often only a narrow strip of habitable land. The mountainous interior, where towering cliffs are interspersed with extensive glacier tables, is largely uninhabited. This explains why Norway, despite its long frontier with Sweden, turns its whole attention westward towards the sea. Shipping and fisheries are the cornerstones of the Norwegian economy.

Since ancient times, the country has been classified in five regions. One is East Norway, with its broad valleys running southwards from the mountainous plateaux in the west and north; this continues along both sides of the Oslo Fjord. Some 50 per cent of the country's arable land and forests lies here. Another is South Norway, the smallest region, which lies fairly high and is crossed by narrower valleys. West Norway forms a third; it has a mountainous interior, is fringed along the coast by precipitous fjords, and is bordered by a chain of thousands of islands. Trøndelag, round the Trondheimfjord, is Norway's most distinctively agricultural region, with forests and iron-mines in the interior. Last comes North Norway, almost all of which lies within the Arctic Circle, a mountainous land split up by countless fjords.

Like Finland, Norway only very recently achieved full political independence, though unlike Finland, she had been independent at an earlier period. The union with Sweden, from 1814 to 1905, and the earlier union with Denmark, from 1380 to 1814, had been preceded by several centuries of national development. Norway was the starting-point of the long voyages made by the Norsemen to France and Ireland; Norwegian emigrants settled in and colonized Iceland, the Faeroes and Greenland.

Basically, the Constitution of 1814 is still in force. Norway is a constitutional, hereditary monarchy, where legislative power is vested in a Parliament (*Storting*) comprising an Upper House (*Lagting*) and a Lower House (*Odelsting*). The established form of worship is that of the Evangelical Lutheran Church, to which 96 per cent of a population of approximately 3,500,000 belong.

134-48 The date of OSLO's foundation (about the year 1050, by King Harald the Hard) makes it the most ancient of the Scandinavian capitals; but the oldest parts of the present city go back no further than the seventeenth century. It was then, after the great fire of 1624, that King Christian IV of Denmark—Norway was linked to Denmark by a 'personal union' from 1380 to 1814—had the town rebuilt and renamed it Christiania. Not until 1925 was the original name restored.

Today Oslo has a population of 477,000, making it by far the largest town in Norway, and is an important trading and industrial centre, with one of Scandinavia's biggest harbours.

135. The fortress of AKERSHUS was founded by Håkon V about 1300. When Oslo was rebuilt in the seventeenth century, this became the nucleus of the town plan.

136. The ROYAL PALACE was built in the years 1825-48, during the reign of Karl Johan Bernadotte, King of Sweden and Norway from 1818-44, in the same Classical style as the University of Uppsala. The monument to N. H. Abel (1802-29), the Norwegian mathematician, is by Gustav Vigeland (cf. pls. 140-3).

137. Oslo UNIVERSITY, founded in 1811, is the focal point of scholarship in Norway; apart from this there is only a small University at Bergen, with three Faculties. The Classical-style main building of Oslo University dates from 1839-54; the lecture theatre, added in 1911, has a cycle of frescoes by Edvard Munch.

138-9. The stern, massive style of the new TOWN HALL, beside the harbour, sets it in characteristic contrast to its Stockholm counterpart (see pl. 97). The design is by two architects, A. Arneberg and M. Poulsson, who won a competition with it in 1917-18 and modernized it before the building actually began, in 1931. The work was interrupted during the war years, and the opening ceremony finally took place in 1950, when Oslo celebrated the ninth centenary of its foundation.

The lavish interior decoration, provided by Norwegian artists, is in keeping with the monumental style of the architecture; the fresco in the main hall (pl. 138) is by Henrik Sörensen (b. 1882) (cf. colour-plate VIII).

140-3. The VIGELAND GARDENS, in the Frogner Park, the north-western district of Oslo. In the course of forty years, Gustav Vigeland (1869-1943) created a Park of Sculpture unique both in concept and in the consistency with which it was carried out. A series of majestically planned sculptural groups in granite and bronze, culminating in a monolith over 55 ft. tall, symbolizes life in its development and decline.

144-5. Of all the thousands of ships that carried the Vikings on their far-flung voyages during the period from A.D. 800 to 1000, only three have survived in more or less complete form. These have been restored and are among the exhibits in the Oldsak Collection at Oslo University. All three were brought on land as burial-ships, and came to light during excavation work beside the Oslo Fjord.

The best preserved is the Oseberg ship, richly carved and stocked with many funeral offerings; the prow and sternpost of this vessel are shown in pls. 144 and 145.

146-7. The BYGDØY Peninsula, in the western part of Oslo, where the Viking ships are on show (cf. pls. 144, 145), is the site of the Norsk Folkemuseum and its large open-air park where old wooden houses have been brought from all over Norway and arranged according to their provinces of origin. One of the exhibits is the ancient barn seen in pl. 146. The medieval (twelfth century) wooden church, brought to Bygdøy from the village of Gol and shown in pl. 147, is one of twenty-five churches which have survived out of several hundred known to have existed. These towering wooden structures, with their skeleton of mast-like wooden pillars and the interior struts which are visible right up into the roof, reached their peak period in the twelfth and thirteenth centuries, after which they made way for stone buildings. The lavish figurative and ornamental carving that decorates many of the stave churches is strongly influenced by pagan ideas inherited from the Viking period (cf. pls. 155, 172, 173).

148. The new residential district of Bøler, on the outskirts of Oslo.

149 KRAGERØ (pop. c. 5,000), a little seaport and popular bathing resort on the south-east coast of Norway.

150-1 The SKJAER-GÅRDEN, a close-set belt of rocky islands, runs almost the entire length of the Norwegian coast. These countless islets and tiny islands show the primeval rock, often with no concealing vegetation (cf. pl. 83). They form an invaluable breakwater for coastal shipping.

152 HAUKELISETER (3,234 ft.), at the eastern end of Lake Stavann, in the mountains of south-west Norway. The Haukeli mountain road forms part of the route from Oslo to Bergen, which goes through the province of Telemark and on by way of Kongsberg, Notodden, Heddal (cf. pl. 155), Haukeligrend and Odda.

153 These carved and painted storehouses are to be seen at Rauland, in the uplands of the province of Telemark, south Norway.

154 This modern church at ULLENSAKER, north-east of Oslo, consecrated in 1958, was designed by Arnstein Arneberg, one of the two architects of the Oslo Town Hall (cf. pls. 138, 139). The frescoes are by Alf Rolfsen, who helped to decorate the Town Hall.

155 The stave church at HEDDAL, near Notodden, in Telemark, is the largest surviving medieval wooden church in Norway (thirteenth century, restored in 1849-51, cf. pl. 147).

156 STAVANGER (pop. c. 55,000) on the Byfjord on the south-west coast of Norway, is one of the oldest towns in the country. It was the seat of a bishopric from the twelfth to the seventeenth century, has a Romanesque Cathedral, and is now an important seaport and a centre of the fish-canning industry.

Nearly all Stavanger's old houses are built of wood, like those shown here which stand on the Holmen Peninsula in the most ancient part of the town.

157 Skis and ski-ing originated in Scandinavia. The earliest known ski, found at Hoting in Sweden, is thought to be 4,500 years old, and the oldest picture of ski-ing, a rock-drawing in northern Norway, dates from about 2000 B.C. The earliest skis were more like rackets in shape and structure; only later were they designed to glide over the snow. They remained purely functional and comparatively primitive in structure until modern sports enthusiasts discovered them. Ski-ing as a sport made its first appearance about 1870, in Norway. The famous ski-jumping competition on the Holmenkollen Redoubt near Oslo was held for the first time in 1892.

The photograph shows the Stuguflaten ski-slopes, near Romsdal.

158 GAUSDAL, in the north of Lillehammer, the chief town of the Opland district, is a favourite winter sports resort. Bjørnstjerne Bjørnson, the poet, had a country house, Aulesstad, near here; it is now a memorial to him, and open to visitors.

159 The River Bjoreia, rushing through a narrow gorge on its way down from the high plateau of Hardangervidda, east of the Hardangerfjord, forms this 535-ft. waterfall, the VØRINGSFOSS.

160 The primeval Scandinavian mountains on the Norwegian coast are cleft by FJORDS which run far inland, many of them branching in different directions. The largest of these lie to the south of Trondheim, the longest of all being the Sognefjord, which extends for about 108 miles. These fjords were originally river

valleys; the glaciers of the Ice Age carved them into deep troughs. In these sea-valleys, sheltered by their high walls of rock and reflected in waters that are usually calm, the climate is appreciably warmer than along the coast.

161-2 Until well into the nineteenth century, BERGEN was the chief town of Norway; it was not until the union with Denmark came to an end, in 1814, that Oslo's rapid development thrust it into second place. Bergen was founded in 1070. It began as a small, insignificant seaport, but by the thirteenth century it had already become the royal residence. Bergen's growth as a powerful trading port and harbour is closely associated with the Hansa, which had a dominating influence there for over two hundred years, from the middle of the fourteenth century until past the middle of the sixteenth. Not until 1760 was the highly efficient Hanseatic counting-house at Bergen finally closed. Modern Bergen, with a population of approximately 120,000, is Norway's second largest town; it has a busy harbour (see pl. 162), thriving industries, and a newly founded University.

161. Most of the wooden houses in the old districts of Bergen have perished in repeated and disastrous outbreaks of fire. Among the survivors are these, on the TYSKE BRYGGEN ('German Bridge'), once the local headquarters of the Hanseatic merchants.

163 The BRIXDALBRE glacier, in the region of the North Fjord, flows down from the Jostedalsbre, the largest glacier field in Europe (nearly 60 miles long). The riven ice-fall of the glacier ends in a small lake.

164 Fertile GUDBRANDSDAL, which extends along both banks of the River Lagen from Lillehammer to Dombas, is Norway's longest valley. Our photograph shows the Eystad Bridge, near Sørfron.

165 Water power is one of Norway's chief natural riches, and supplies the whole country with electricity at a comparatively low cost.
This aerial photograph shows the AURSUND, with one of the 2,000 power-stations which Norway possesses.

166 The BUARBRE, a large glacier near Odda, in Hardanger.

167 Lake VÅGÅ, in the north of the Jotunheimen mountains (cf. pl. 168) lies in a typical ex-glacier valley, trough-shaped in the foreground and sinking to a deeply indented U in the part now filled by water.

168 JOTUNHEIMEN, the 'Home of the Giants', with an average altitude of approximately 6,560 ft., is the highest mountain range in northern Europe and includes Scandinavia's loftiest peaks (Galdhøpiggen, 8,095 ft., and Glittertind, 8,043 ft.). Wrapped in clouds in the background is the Skagastølstinder massif.

169 The MOLDEFJORD, north-east of Ålesund, is an unusually broad arm of the sea which, as it makes its way inland, divides into a number of narrow fjords, including the Langfjord and the Romsdalsfjord. In the foreground is an old mill-house. Although the Moldefjord lies far to the north, its sheltered position allows of remarkably lavish vegetation, with copper-beech, ash, lime trees, etc.

170-1 SVARTISEN, on the Arctic Circle, and FROSTISEN, south of Narvik, are two of the most extensive ancient snowfields in northern Norway. Plate 170 shows clearly the contrast between the hills in the foreground, worn smooth and furrowed by the glaciers of the Ice Age, and the angular 'Alps' and sharp peaks of the older mountains above glacier level.

172-3 The stave church at BORGUND on the Laerdalselv, to the east of the Sognefjord (mid twelfth century) is considered to be the best preserved of Norway's medieval wooden churches, while that at Urnes on the Lusterfjord passes for the most ancient. The dragon heads on the ridge-turrets at Borgund, with their outstretched necks, are reminiscent of the Viking ships (cf. pls. 144, 145), while the carved doorway at URNES (pl. 173) reminds us that the Vikings were highly skilled woodcarvers.

174 RØROS (pop. c. 3,000), south-east of Trondheim and not far from the frontier of Sweden, was founded in 1644, after the discovery of the local copper deposits which are still being worked today. The church, round which the mining village huddles, was built in 1780.

175 The Romsdal, between Dombas and Andalsnes on the Romsdalsfjord, continues the Gudbrandsdal in a north-westerly direction. It is one of the most beautiful of Norway's inland valleys, hemmed in by cliffs which at some points form almost vertical precipices. TROLL-TINDENE (the 'Trolls' Peaks', 5,900 ft.) are among the highest points of the Romsdal.

176-7 TRONDHEIM (pop. c. 60,000) is the third largest town in Norway. For a great part of the Middle Ages, when it went by the name of Nidaros, it was the country's biggest and most powerful city. Its eleventh-century founder, King Olav the Saint, was buried there, and until the Reformation it remained a religious centre, a favourite place of pilgrimage, a lively trading town, and at times the royal residence. It stands in a sheltered position in the Trondheimfjord, and has an excellent harbour and flourishing industries.

176. View across the NIDELV, which flows in a wide loop round the old district of Trondheim, to a group of warehouses and the spire of the Cathedral.

177. The Cathedral, the finest church in Scandinavia in design and execution, was founded in the latter half of the eleventh century as a burial-place for King Olav the Saint, and considerably enlarged during the twelfth century, on English lines; the early Gothic octagonal tower dates from this period. In the course of centuries the Cathedral was damaged and repaired several times, the last being in 1870–1930, when far-reaching restorations were carried out. As laid down in the Constitution, all Norwegian kings have been crowned here since 1814.

178 BODØ (pop. c. 8,000), which lies within the Arctic Circle, at the mouth of the Saltfjord, is an important herring-fishing port. It was almost completely destroyed during the Second World War, and has since been rebuilt.

179 NARVIK (pop. c. 12,000), which stands on a peninsula in the Ofotfjord, is the terminus of the Lapland railway and, being never blocked by ice, serves as a permanent port of lading for the Swedish iron ore from Kiruna and Gällivare. This is loaded without interruption throughout the day and night into the ships that lie at the up-to-date wharfs, rebuilt after their destruction during the war (centre of picture).

180 These sharp ribs of primeval (Cambro-Silurian) rock-strata are to be seen on the SALTFJORD, near Bodø. At top right of the picture we see one of the beach-terraces thrown up in parts of Scandinavia after the Ice Age (cf. pls. 82, 83).

181–6 The LOFOTEN ISLANDS, separated from the mainland by the wide Vestfjord, together with the Vesteralen, form an archipelago off the coast of north Norway, between latitude 68° and latitude 70°. The four large islands—Austvagøy, Vestvagøy, Moskenesøy and Flakstadøy—with a few smaller ones, form a 90-mile chain extending far into the ocean (500 sq. miles), rising in places to a height of 4,100 ft. above sea-level, with many bays and fjords whose precipitous cliffs may be well over 3,000 ft. high. The climate is damp, but for such a northerly position the winters are extraordinarily mild. The larger islands are surrounded by a host of rocky islets (pl. 181).

182–5. The Vestfjord fishing grounds are among the richest in the world. During the high season, from January to April, huge shoals of codfish come to spawn along the coast. The fish are cut open or split in half and hung to dry on wooden frames, where they remain until June (pl. 185), or salted and spread out on the rocks; afterwards they are stored in great, covered heaps. The Lofoten Islands have a certain share in the whaling industry (pl. 184), but the principal base of the large Norwegian whaling fleet, which now operates chiefly in the Antarctic, is the Vestfold area, on the Oslofjord.

187 Norway and Sweden are connected by a ferro-concrete bridge spanning the narrow SVINESUND at a height of 213 ft.

188 Looking across the SØRØYSUND, south of Hammerfest, the northernmost town in the world, with the islands of Haja and Hjelmen showing as dusky silhouettes in the late evening light.

189 The Korken, in Norfold, south of Narvik, rising to a height of 3,716 ft.

190 The 1,007 ft. high NORTH CAPE, latitude 71° 10′ 20″, rises, a slaty mass, at the northern tip of Magerøy Island, and is generally accepted as the northernmost point of Europe, though Cape Knivskjelodden projects slightly further northwards.

191–3 SVALBARD was the name given in 1925 to the administrative district of Norway which comprises the Spitsbergen archipelago, Bear Island and various smaller islands in the Arctic Ocean.

Spitsbergen (23,668 sq. miles) was first discovered from Iceland at the end of the twelfth century. However, its existence was afterwards forgotten, until it was rediscovered, once and for all, by the Dutchman, Willem Barents, in 1596. For centuries it had no more than a seasonal population of whale fishers and fur-hunters, most of whom were Russians or Norwegians. Norway's sovereignty over the islands was finally recognized in the Treaty of Sèvres (1920). Spitsbergen's geological strata range from primeval rock to the tertiary period. The islands are covered to a great extent by glaciers—54 per cent of the surface of the largest island, Vestspitsbergen, and 77 per cent of that of Nordaustlandet being under ice.

Most of the fjords end in a glacier precipice varying

in height from 98 to 164 ft. (pl. 191). The aerial photograph given here (pl. 193), looking southwards, clearly shows the glacier formation on the north side of the two parallel valleys, while the retreating ice on the southern slopes has already melted. The terminal, medial and lateral moraines of the individual glaciers are easily distinguishable.

Spitsbergen's coalfields have been worked since the beginning of the present century by companies of various nationalities, including one Russian (pl. 192). About 1,200 people remain during the winter at Longyearbyen, the largest Norwegian settlement. Most of the coal lies in almost horizontal seams, about 3 ft. to 3 ft. 4 in. deep, in the hills high above the valley bottom, and can be extracted with no risk of flooding, since the rock is frozen to a great depth. Exports (other than Russian) amount to between 400,000 and 500,000 tons per annum.

GREENLAND

Plates 194–199

Greenland is the largest island in the world. But of its total area of 840,000 sq. miles, all but 131,930 sq. miles is covered with ice, leaving a coastal strip, narrow in most places, with a population of about 30,000, the majority of which is concentrated in the south-west.

Greenland was colonized by Norsemen as early as the year 1000, but about five hundred years later the European settlers were wiped out, losing their stubborn battle against the climate and the Eskimo penetration. The modern European settlement of Greenland began in 1721, with the missionary activity of a Danish clergyman, Hans Egede (1686–1758), who established a colony at Godthåb, now the principal town on the island. Until 1953 Greenland ranked as a Danish colony; since then it has had equality of status with Denmark. The economy is based on fishing and fish-processing; fresh prospects for this industry have been opened up by the great influx of codfish into Greenland waters as a result of recent changes in the climate, which is growing milder.

195 True ESKIMOS are rare in Greenland, the great majority of the population being of mixed Eskimo and European stock. Some of the inhabitants, chiefly those living in the north, still follow their original pursuit, seal-hunting, but most of them nowadays earn a living by fishing, working in the fish industry, or sheep-rearing.

196–8 From the gigantic inland masses, the maximum depth of which is 6,560 ft. and the average depth 4,970 ft., the ice forces its way through gaps in the surrounding mountains and flows down in huge glaciers towards the sea. On reaching the coast or the shores of the countless fjords, the ice either melts or breaks up into fragments which drift away as icebergs into the open sea.

199 The traditional KAYAK has been largely replaced by modern forms of sea transport, and hunting with a harpoon from a kayak (pl. 199) is no longer an important activity. The boat is covered with sealskin except for one small opening which is filled up and hermetically sealed by the occupant's bulk.

FINLAND

Plates 200–225

Finland (its name in the Finnish language is Suomi—land of lakes and bogs) is one of the most northerly countries in the world. It lies between latitude 59° and 70° north and between longitude 19° and 31° east, and is bordered by Norway, Sweden and the USSR. Its heavily indented sea-coast along the Gulfs of Finland and Bothnia is about 960 miles long and is fringed with a line of rocky islands. Finland has a total area of 130,116 sq. miles, of which some 11,600 sq. miles are covered by lakes—numbering over 60,000—while about 60 per cent of the country consists of forest. Its greatest length from north to south is 696 miles, of which about one-third lies within the Arctic Circle.

Geologically and morphologically, Finland forms part of Fennoskandia, the vast stretch of crystalline rocks dating from the remotest ages of the earth and consisting chiefly of granite and gneiss, which includes Norway, Sweden, Finland, the Kola Peninsula and Russian Karelia. Finland's basic rock formation consists of a peneplain averaging 328–656 ft. above sea-level which occasionally, in the north-west of the country, rises to or above 3,200 ft. The Ice Age left Finland covered with an extensive but usually shallow network of moraines, including a few high ridges such as the double wall of the Salpausselkä, which forms the southern limit of the lake district of central Finland.

Height above sea-level increases from the fertile coastal plains of south Finland, through the lake district, to the borders of Lapland.

The Finns, originally a tribe living on the eastern shores of the Baltic, moved northwards into their present territory at about the beginning of the Christian era. Only since 1917 has Finland been an independent Republic, with a democratic, parliamentary constitution. At that time, in the confusion induced by the Russian Revolution, the Finns managed to shake off the suzerainty exercised by the Russians since the conclusion of the Finnish War of 1809. Before that, Finland had been a Swedish province for 650 years, always under the threat of the recurrent wars between Sweden and Russia. Of today's 4,500,000 inhabitants (average population density 34 per sq. mile), 350,000 are still Swedish-speaking.

200 The lake of KILPISJÄRVI (15 sq. miles, 1,529 ft. above sea-level) lies in the extreme north-west of Finnish Lapland, in a narrow strip of Finnish territory not far from the point where Finland, Sweden and Norway meet. The hills in the background are on Swedish territory.

201-4 LAPLAND, which slopes in a gentle declivity from west to east, comprises the northern areas of Norway, Sweden and Finland and the Soviet territory of Karelia. The Lapps, numbering about 35,000, make up one-tenth of the population of this region—the majority of them, perhaps 20,000, living in Norway. They came here from further east at an early period, and were originally nomadic, with reindeer-breeding as their only source of revenue. In course of time some of them settled down as fishers and farmers—a development which has recently been assisted by the State and is now rapidly accelerating. The State also provides schools for the Lapp children (pl. 204).

201-3. The REINDEER are the essential factor in the lives of those Lapps who are still nomadic—supplying them with food and clothing, transport and a source of income. In Scandinavia as a whole, the reindeer number several hundred thousand. At the end of each big migration, the beasts are driven into a great enclosure and sorted out by their respective owners, like sheep in Iceland (cf. pl. 9). It takes great skill and strength to lasso a reindeer (pl. 202).

205-6 Trees and water are the dominant features of the Finnish landscape (cf. pls. 220, 223, 225).

207 The village of HATTULA, north of Hämeenlinna in southern Finland, possesses one of the most ancient stone-built churches in the country; the oldest parts of it stand on the site of a mid-thirteenth-century wooden church and date from the early fourteenth century. It has numerous frescoes, the earliest of which were painted in the middle of the fifteenth century.

208 TURKU (known to the Swedes as Åbo; pop. c. 125,000, about 10 per cent of whom are Swedish-speaking) stands at the mouth of the Aurajoki, in south-west Finland; it is the country's oldest and third largest town. Originally a trading-post of the pre-Christian period, Turku developed into the region's principal seaport, became an episcopal see, a University town (1640) and the capital of the country until 1812, when, Finland having passed into Russian possession in 1809, the government was transferred to Helsinki, where the University followed it in 1828.

In 1827, Turku was almost entirely destroyed by fire, but was subsequently rebuilt under the direction of Carl Ludwig Engel. Despite all these blows, Turku remained an important economic and cultural centre.

The medieval wooden statue of St Anne with the Virgin and Child comes from Turku Cathedral (built in the thirteenth century and several times restored), but is now in the city's Historical Museum.

209 SAVONLINNA (pop. c. 15,000), situated between Lakes Haapavesi and Pihlajavesi, in the lake district of Saimaa, south-east Finland, is a popular health and foreign tourist resort, built partly on islands. It owes its origin to Olavinlinna (Olaf's Castle), which stands on a small island near by (pl. 209), one of the best preserved medieval fortresses in Scandinavia. This was built in 1457-77 by a Dane—E. A. Tott, of Viborg, who commanded it—to guard the province of Savo against attack from the east. During the Great Nordic War it fell to Russia, was afterwards occupied for a time by a Swedish garrison, but finally passed to Russia by the Peace of Turku. Damaged by fire, it was extensively restored in 1872-7.

210-14 HELSINKI was founded by Gustav Vasa in 1550; the Swedish King wished to establish a trading post which could compete with the mercantile towns on the south side of the Gulf of Finland. It failed to develop according to expectations, owing to the unfavourable position of the original site, $5\frac{1}{2}$ miles north-east of what is now the city's centre, and in 1639 it was moved to the Vironniemi Peninsula, with its deep inlets and granite-hummocked surface. Helsinki did not become a really important city until the first half of the nineteenth century—after 1812, when it replaced Turku as the capital of the autonomous Grand-Duchy of Finland, which had been under Russian suzerainty since 1809. In 1918, after the successful conclusion of the Finnish war of independence, Helsinki became the capital of the Republic of Finland.

Today, with a population of over 460,000, about a quarter of which is Swedish-speaking, Helsinki is the administrative and cultural nucleus of Finland, with important industries, and the centre of the country's import trade.

210. In the early nineteenth century, Helsinki's architectural and urban development was supervised by a Building Committee, with the statesman and architect Albert Ehrenström as its chairman and the architect Carl Ludwig Engel (1778–1840), of Berlin, as Ehrenström's adviser. Engel was a pupil of Schinkel and endowed Helsinki with many neo-Classical buildings of high artistic quality, including the SUURKIRKKO (Great Church). This church was erected in the years 1830–52; it looks down from a granite terrace upon the square where the Senate stands, as part of Engel's homogeneous design. In the middle of the square is a statue of Alexander II.

211. The UNIVERSITY LIBRARY (Yliopiston Kirjasto), on the western side of the Senate square (cf. pl. 210) was built to Engel's design in 1836–45.

212–14. The OLYMPIC STADIUM at Helsinki, with its 236-ft. tower, was built in 1938, to the designs of Yrjö Lindgren and Toivo Jäntti, for the 1940 Olympic Games, which were cancelled because of the war. The Olympics were not held at Helsinki until 1952.

215–17 ALVAR AALTO, the well-known Finnish architect, has won international celebrity with his buildings in Europe and overseas. These three photographs illustrate his methods of dealing with three different problems—the 'Church with three Crosses', at Vuoksenniska, in the Imatra district of south-east Finland (215), the Town Hall on Säynätsalo (216) and a country house on Muuratsalo (217), two islands in Lake Päijänne, south Finland.

218–19 Social welfare measures, such as the public health system and housing construction, are highly developed in Finland, and run on up-to-date lines. Plate 218 shows a CHILDREN'S HOME and pl. 219 a HOUSING ESTATE in the vicinity of Helsinki.

220 Some 24,000 miles of natural waterways—rivers and innumerable lakes—facilitate the transport of the vast quantities of timber annually felled in Finland. The trunks are either floated down separately or, on the lakes, roped together into great rafts and towed along.

221 A COTTAGE in KARELIA. Karelia lies in the low ground between the Gulf of Finland and the White Sea. By the last cession of Finnish territory, in 1940, it passed entirely into Russian hands, but it originally formed a natural part of the area inhabited by the Finnish-speaking people. Eastern Karelia had belonged to Russia since the Middle Ages. Many refugees from the ceded areas made their way to Finland and found a new home there.

222 In a SAUNA. 'The Sauna is an indispensable feature of every farm, not only as a bath-place, but as a lying-in room for the farmer's and cottagers' wives. Yes, a steaming bath-house, a barking dog, a crowing cock and a mewing cat are the tokens of a good farmhouse!' So says Juhani in *Seven Brothers*, by Aleksis Kivi, adding that the Sauna 'with its sizzling steam is the only happiness of the poor'. The life of the country people in Finland begins in the Sauna, and to it they retire in extreme old age. It is much more than a place for physical cleansing; it is a place where strangers become brothers.

223 View from the Koli Mountains in south-east Finland, looking across Lake Pielinen towards the Russian frontier.

224 The KANTELE, the Finnish zither which is carved out of a single block of wood, survives as an example of an ancient type of pluck-stringed instrument.
This old Karelian peasant, in the Koli district, is playing one that he made himself.

225 Finland is one of the world's largest timber-producing countries: 60 per cent of its total area is covered with forest, 55 per cent of the trees being firs, 30 per cent spruce and 14 per cent silver birch. Sweden's timber reserves are even more extensive, but this raw material plays a much greater part in the economic life of Finland. Wood and wood products form the major part of its exports, from timber to its final industrial forms (paper, furniture). Some 40 million cubic metres of timber are felled each year—chiefly in winter, when 200,000 men go to work in the forests.

INDEX OF PLACES

ACKNOWLEDGEMENTS

Aalto, Alvar, Helsinki (through Verlag Girsberger, Zürich), 215–17

Aistrup, Inga, Copenhagen, 20, 29, 40, 46, 50, 51, 53–5, 57, 59–61, 63, 67, 69

Bernild, Bror, 68

Bischof, Werner (Magnum), 200, 204–8, 214, 218, 221–4

Böklin, Lena, 110

Bräm, Jakob (Conzett & Huber, Zürich), VI

Brenneisen, M. (Dr. Hans Stauber, Zürich), 196

Dittmer, Harry (Tio, Stockholm), 121

Ehrhardt, Alfred, Hamburg, 6

Fietz, Helga (Bavaria, Gauting vor München), 10

Gardi, René, Bern, 181, 184–6, 191, 192, 202, 203, 220

Gillsäter, Sven (Tio, Stockholm), 125, 126

Gullers, Karl, 182

Gunner, Dan, Stockholm, 113

Hansson, Gunnar, Örnsköldsvik, 83, 115, 122, 123, 132, 133

Haven, Mogens von, Copenhagen, 30, 37

Hofer, Ernst, Bern (Koch-Expedition, Copenhagen), 197

Hürlimann, Dr. Martin, Zürich, I, V, VII, 21–5, 27, 31–6, 38, 41–4, 92, 94–8, 100–7, 134–47

Jespersen, Aage, Byen, 194

Karlsson, Bror, 91

Klages, Jürg, Zürich, 211, 225

Koehn, Henry, Kampen, 18, 19

Lüden, Walter, Hamburg, 56, 58, 66

Lüthy, W. (Bavaria), 198, 199

Malmberg, Hans (Tio, Stockholm), 108

Marquis, Jean (Len Sirman Press, Geneva), 201

Maurer, F., Zürich, 210, 212, 213, 219

Mittet Foto, Oslo, 150, 151, 154, 158, 159, 166, 167, 183, 187, 190

Nilsson, Pal-Nils (Tio, Stockholm), 77, 87, 120

Nordin, Gösta, Stockholm, 127, 130

Oddner, Georg (Tio, Stockholm), 71

Olson, Lennart (Tio, Stockholm), 73–6, 119

Refot, Stockholm, 72, 81, 84, 109, 111, 112, 116–18

Royal Reklamfoto, Stockholm, 99

Schlenker, Hermann, Schwenningen II, III, 1–9, 11–17, 195

Schneiders, Toni, Lindau I, IV, 26, 28, 39, 45, 47–9, 52, 62, 64, 70, 78, 79, 82, 86, 88, 89, 93, 114, 124, 128, 129, 131, 152, 153, 155, 156, 160–4, 168, 169, 171–80, 189

Süddeutscher Verlag (Photo archive), 157, 188, 209

Svenska Turisttrafikförbundet, Stockholm
Kung. Vattenfallsstryrelsen, 80
E. Lundin, 85
P. v. Wahlgren, 90

Thoby, Sven, Copenhagen, 65

Widerøe's Flyveselskap, Oslo, 148, 149, 165, 170
Forsvarsstaben, 193

HAÍFOSS

HÚSAVÍK

2

REYKJAVÍK

3

HVERAGERDI

HVERAGERDI. GRÝTA

ÖXNADALUR

6

TORFBAER

7

VESTMANNAEYIAR

RÉTTIR

DREGID Í DILKA 10

SIGLUF JÖRDUR

HJÁ SELFOSSI

SKÓGAFOSS

13

SELVEIDIMENN

LANDMANNALAUGAR

SÚLNASKER

FÖROYAR

FÖROYAR

FANØ

KØBENHAVN. MARMORKIRKE

KØBENHAVN. AMALIENBORG

KØBENHAVN. AMALIENBORG

KØBENHAVN. KNIPPELSBRO

KØBENHAVN. STRANDGADE 25

KØBENHAVN. BØRSEN 26

KØBENHAVN. FRELSERS KIRKE

KØBENHAVN. GRUNDTVIGKIRKE

KØBENHAVN, TIVOLI

KØBENHAVN. DEN KONGELIGE BALLET

KØBENHAVN. GAMMEL STRAND

KØBENHAVN. NYBODER

KØBENHAVN. DEN LILLE HAVFRUE

KØBENHAVN. KONGENS HAVE, H. C. ANDERSEN

KØBENHAVN. SAS ROYAL HOTEL

KØBENHAVN-BELLAHØJ

FRILANDMUSEET VED KØBENHAVN

SKAGEN

VEDERSØ

KRONBORG

HELSINGØR

FREDENSBORG   44

FREDERIKSBORG   45

EGESKOV SLOT

ROSKILDE

ROSKILDE. DOMKIRKE

48

KALUNDBORG

BJERNEDE. KIRKE

MØENS-KLINT

ODENSE

LØGUMKLOSTER

BERRITSGÅRD

SPØTTRUP

STEVNS

RANDERS

ÅLBORG-LINDHØLM

VEJLE. RUNESTEN

RIBE. DOMKIRKE 64

ÅRHUS. UNIVERSITET 65

ÅRHUS

FANØ. VESTERHAUSBAD 67

ØRESUND 68

MALMÖ

MALMÖ 71

GÖTEBORG 72

GÖTEBORG

GÖTEBORG

HÄLSINGBORG 75

LANDSKRONA 76

KALMAR

LUND

VADSTENA

STRÄNGNÄS

BOHUSLÄN

BOHUSLÄN

VISBY

VISBY

ÖLAND

GOTSKA SANDÖN

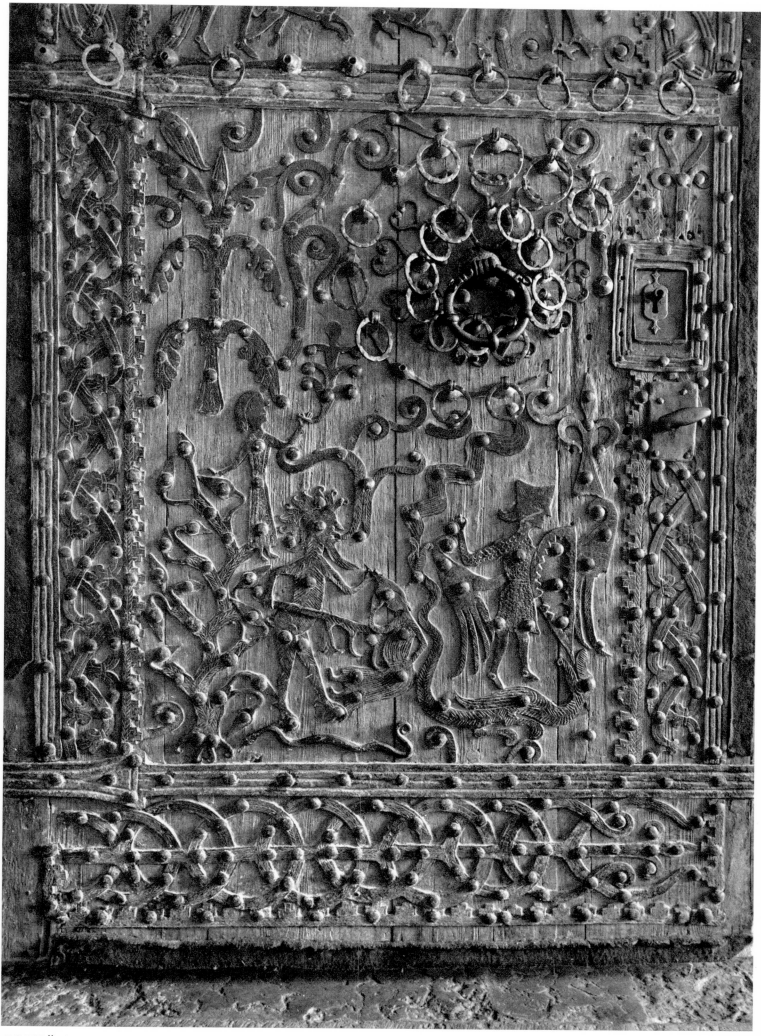

ROGSLÖSA

STORA VÄRTAN

SIGTUNA

STOCKHOLM. WASA-SKEPPET

STOCKHOLM. KUNGLIGA SLOTTET   92

STOCKHOLM. VAKTPARADEN   93

STOCKHOLM. STORKYRKAN

STOCKHOLM. RIKSDAGSHUSET

STOCKHOLM. SLUSSEN

STOCKHOLM. STADSHUSET

STOCKHOLM. RIDDARHOLMEN

VÄLLINGBY

STOCKHOLM. MILLESGÅRDEN

om Bröllöpret i cåana i gallileen. där Jesus bende watten i wi

nya år M3 Jungfru marie BeBodelse M3 Udam och Eva Gynbade M3

DROTTNINGHOLM

UPPSALA

GAMLA UPPSALA

ROTTNEROS HERGÅRD

MÅRBACKA

ROSLAGSBRO

117

MALMGRUVA

BLEKINGE. KARLSHAMNS OLJEFABRIKER

SOMMARMORGON I NORDSVERIGE

HÄLSINGLAND

TRÄ

SÖRLEVIKEN

HÄLSINGLAND

HÄLSINGLAND

ÅNGERMANLAND

KIRUNA

OSLO

134

OSLO. AKERSHUS FESTNING

135

OSLO. KGL. SLOTTET OG ABEL-STATUEN

OSLO. UNIVERSITETET 137

OSLO. RÅDHUSET 138

OSLO. RÅDHUSET

OSLO. VIGELAND-ANLEGGET   140

OSLO. VIGELAND-ANLEGGET   141

OSLO. VIGELAND-ANLEGGET 142

OSLO. VIGELAND-ANLEGGET 143

OSLO. VIKINGSKIPENE

144

145

OSLO. NORSK FOLKEMUSEUM

OSLO. NORSK FOLKEMUSEUM

BØDER

KRAGERØ

FRA SKJÆRGÅRDEN   150

FRA SKJÆRGÅRDEN   151

HAUKELISETER

RAULAND

ULLENSAKER

HEDDAL

STAVANGER

SKILØPERE

ÖSTRE GAUSDAL

VØRINGSFOSS

BERGEN

BRIXDALBRE

GUDBRANDSDALEN   164

AURSUNDEN   165

BUARBRE

VÅGÅ FJORD

JOTUNHEIMEN

MOLDEFJORD

SVARTISEN

FROSTISEN

RØROS

TRONDHEIM

TRONDHEIM

BODØ

NARVIK

SALTFJORD

LOFOTEN

LOFOTEN

LOFOTEN

LOFOTEN

LOFOTEN 186

SVINESUND 187

SØRØYSUNDET

188

KORGEN

NORDKAP

SPITSBERGEN/SVALBARD

SPITSBERGEN/SVALBARD

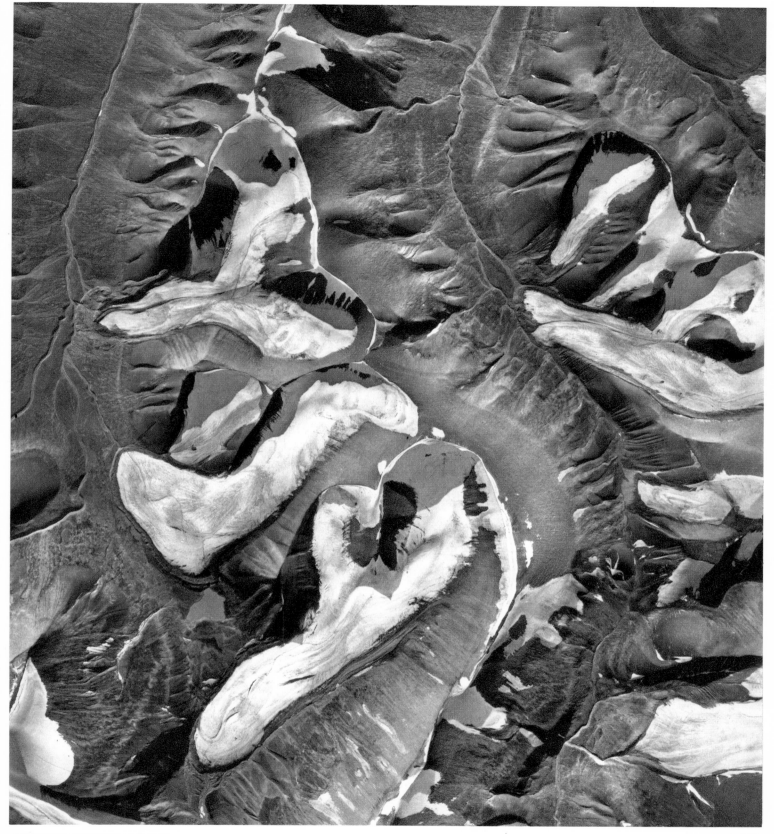

SPITSBERGEN/SVALBARD

GRØNLAND 194

GRØNLAND 195

GRØNLAND

GRØNLAND

KILPISJÄRVI

PORON

POROLAJITTELU

POROTOKKA

LAPPALAISIA

HAKKUNALUE

TUKINUITTO

HATTULA

SAVONLINNA

HELSINKI. SUURKIRKKO

HELSINKI. YLIOPISTON KIRJASTO

HELSINKI. STADION

HELSINKI. STADION

HELSINKI. STADION

VUOKSENNISKA

SÄYNÄTSALO

216

MUURATSALO

217

LASTEN PARANTOLA

HELSINKI

TUKKILAUTTA

SAUNA

KOLI

KANTELEENSOITTAJA

METSÄ